T0323211

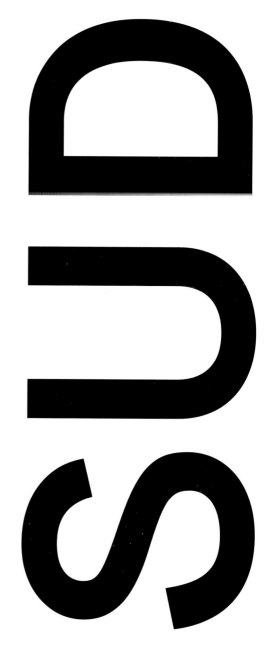

LE SUD

RECIPES FROM
PROVENCE–ALPES–CÔTE D'AZUR

REBEKAH PEPPLER
Photographs by **Joann Pai**

CHRONICLE BOOKS
SAN FRANCISCO

Text copyright © 2024 by Rebekah Peppler.
Photographs copyright © 2024 by Joann Pai.
Illustrations copyright © 2024 by Iris Marchand and Rebekah Peppler.

All rights reserved. No part of this book may be reproduced
in any form without written permission from the publisher.

Library of Congress Cataloging-in-Publication Data available.

ISBN 978-1-7972-1953-0

Manufactured in China.

Food and prop styling by Rebekah Peppler.
Illustrations by Iris Marchand and Rebekah Peppler.
Additional research by Laila Said.
Design by Lizzie Vaughan.

From the photographer: Thank you to the best team! I'm so lucky we
get to create together. To B for being my béton, I love you like a mofo.

10 9 8 7 6 5 4 3 2

Chronicle books and gifts are available at special quantity discounts to
corporations, professional associations, literacy programs, and other
organizations. For details and discount information, please contact
our premiums department at corporatesales@chroniclebooks.com
or at 1-800-759-0190.

Chronicle Books LLC
680 Second Street
San Francisco, California 94107
www.chroniclebooks.com

para laila

INTRODUCTION

The thing is, all the clichés you've heard about the south of France are true. The light takes on new forms by the hour, casting beauty on the simplest pleasures. There are open-air markets bursting with sun-ripened produce; the surprisingly loud, surprisingly comforting surround-sound of cicadas in late summer; acres of olive trees, lavender, and sunflowers; cliffs that drop into salt-heavy turquoise coves. And the food? It's not overrated. The figs, the ratatouille, the aïoli, the crispy panisse, pissaladière, braids of garlic, Provençal melons, an overwhelming variety of local cheeses, actually good tapenades, and all the rest.

This is the part of France where the French themselves holiday. It is where throngs of Europeans descend for summer vacances—doing their best French cosplay while lounging, flirting, apéro-ing in the sun. American in Paris, yes yes sure, but the south is no stranger to American expats, of which I am just one in a steady line. M.F.K., Child, Jones, Wells, and many more fell for the charms of le sud, gravitating to the sea and countryside alike for some swirl of inspiration, relaxation, hedonism, and escapism, and, ultimately, to try their hand at capturing a bit of its enchantment on the page.

BUT. The southeastern region of France known as Provence-Alpes-Côte d'Azur isn't solely a fantasyland of wine and lavender and endless vacation. It's a real place, with real people and four seasons.

The 12,000 square miles (or 31,000 square kilometers, if you will) that make up Provence-Alpes-Côte d'Azur are bounded in the north by the snowcapped Southern Alps and in the south by the blue French Mediterranean. The Italian border (and its culinary influence, of course) marks the east; the Rhône River makes up its western edge. Included within its borders are vineyards, olive groves, pine forests, lavender fields, the Camargue plains and marshes, rivers, and the Mediterranean seaside. Influences from Mediterranean and African countries arrived and were absorbed via modern trade and travel, colonization, migration, and exile. The region's food culture is made—first and foremost—in the home, reflecting and drawing directly from the region's people and landscapes. The resulting recipes translate the region's terroir onto the plate while veering away from overwrought, technique-heavy dishes that tend to be associated with French haute cuisine.

What you can expect in the book you're holding is a small piece of this region's story, which hopefully captures larger ideas about this region's story. And I think some of my own story wrapped within. All through the lens of the Provençal table. Or tables, varied as they are.

Beyond the postcard and outside the superficial lies an abundant, golden-lit reality. Since moving to Paris, I've spent . . . a lot of time and energy finding ways to be in this special part of France's south.

While researching my first book, *Apéritif*, I took a sometimes liberating, sometimes excruciatingly solo road trip from Forcalquier in Haute Provence, through Aix-en-Provence and Chateâurenard, down the Mediterranean coast and outside Provence's proverbial borders to Banyuls-sur-Mer, just short of the Spanish border, eating and drinking and pushing my linguistic comfort zone the entire way.

I wrote a bunch of the recipes in my second book, *À Table*, in friends' kitchens and sparsely equipped rentals in le sud. Do I now travel with a cutting board? Yes. Sharp knives? Also yes. We shot part of that book in the hills and cobblestone streets of the Luberon. We came back and shot part of this book there too, and also in and around Marseille and at Julia Child's former holiday home near Grasse. I drank a lot of rosé on a birthday spent on the red rocks of Saint-Raphaël and another in sunflower fields outside Cavaillon. And another yet in the Calanques near Cassis, lounging pretty uncomfortably, tbh, on pebble beaches, snacking on sun-warmed fruit and potato chips and chickpea salad (page 209), watching braver souls than I cliff jump. (Something about me is that I am a double Cancer and I will *do* my birthday.)

I've taken the train out of Gare de Lyon to toast friends who have opened restaurants from Saint-Saturnin-lès-Apt to Arles—a city loved by van Gogh and M.F.K. Fisher and that now also holds a piece of my heart. I spent a French take on Thanksgiving in charming Eygalières. I've fallen in love anew with both rice and salt, each farmed in the marshy Camargue region unique to Provence.

During a lengthy recovery with long COVID, I spent a month in La Ciotat—a port city on the Mediterranean coast near Bandol—gingerly assimilating into the weekday regulars at the small beach and attempting to heal through a combination of sea air, fresh figs, and end-of-season tomatoes. It helped. I found myself back in La Ciotat a few years later while working on the edits for this book. Suffice to say, I started my research—and accompanying stories—for this book the moment I moved to France in 2015 and don't plan on stopping anytime soon.

Provence-Alpes-Côte d'Azur cooking is country cooking and city cooking and seaside cooking and mountain cooking and river cooking. And like so many regions where landscapes happily crash into each other in this way, the food is dynamic, it's exciting, it's new and it's old, and maybe needless to say at this point, all things considered—it's very worth writing a book about.

Bon baiser du sud,
RKP

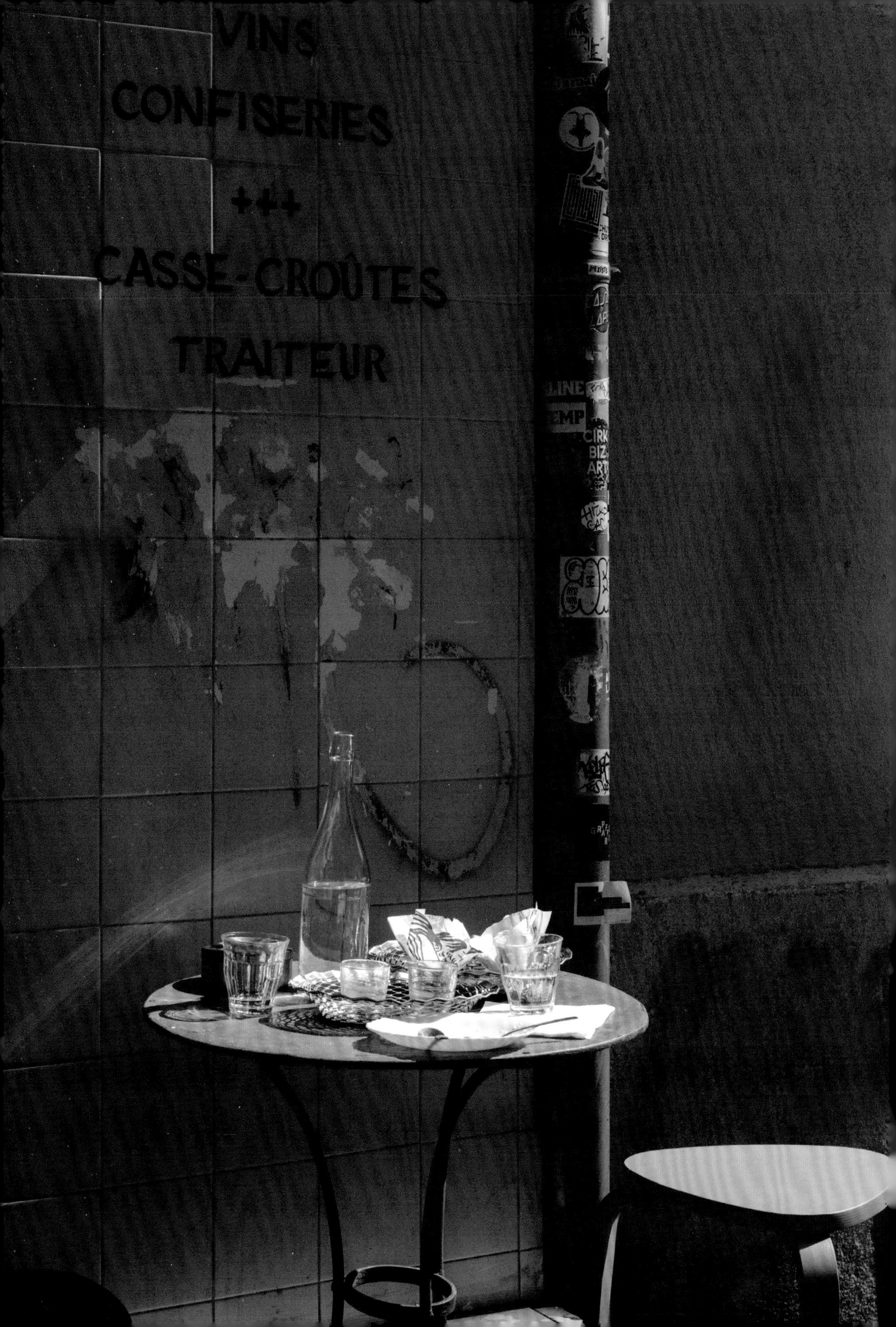
VINS
CONFISERIES
+++
CASSE-CROÛTES
TRAITEUR

A NOTE ON ITALICS

This book, written by an English speaker and published by an American publishing house, includes French words and phrases throughout the text in an effort to inform, provide color, or deepen the reader's understanding of my personal experience in the country I call home. While a translation and/or explanation for these inclusions is often provided with an eye toward clarity, *le SUD* does not follow what has been the standard practice of italicizing non-English words.

This shift may require a small lift from English-speaking readers who, after years of conditioning, need a moment to readjust to a style that doesn't frame English as the dominant language. To readers who have a working knowledge of French, I hope this stylistic shift furthers and provides fluidity to your experience of reading two languages side by side. To those who rightfully question why I'm taking this particular stand with French—a language and culture that has often and readily contributed to the colonization and othering of cultures and peoples around the world—I say this: We can only start where we are.

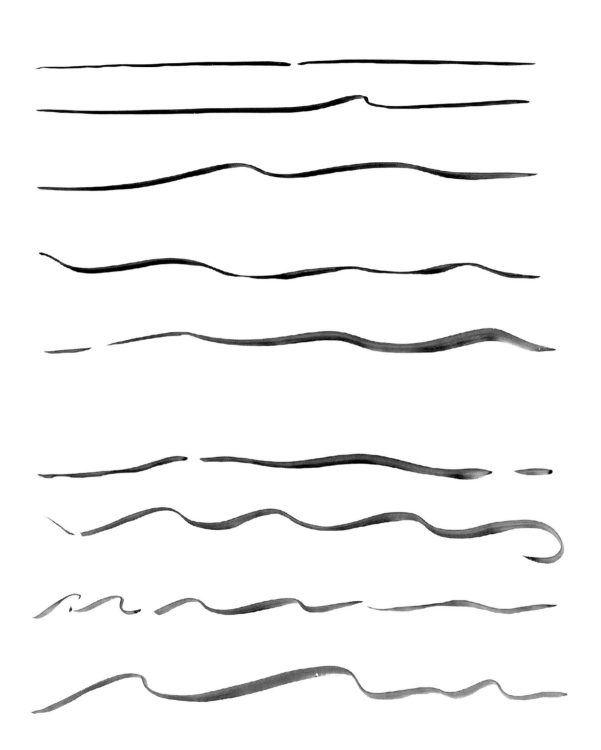

to START

TO START

DRINKING

La Piscine

In French, *piscine* means *pool*. And that, mon ami, is where this tale begins—around a rented one just outside the tiny Provençal village of Maillane with a few friends, just shy of my thirtieth, freshly out of the closet, and holding the life-affirming weight that is a glass full of wine and ice. In le sud, I was reborn.

For 1

Fill a wine glass with ice cubes and top with the wine. Serve immediately.

5 ounces [150 ml] dry sparkling wine, such as Champagne, crémant, or pétillant naturel, or dry sparkling or still rosé

La Grande Plage

No shade but *this* is the spritz to make when you're by the sea (or want to be) and desire something lightly bitter and bubbly and giving sunset in a cup.

For 1

In a wine glass filled with ice, combine the Lillet, amaro, bitters, and salt. Top with the sparkling wine. Add the citrus wheels directly in the glass (if using) and serve.

1½ ounces [45 ml] Lillet Rosé

¾ ounce [22.5 ml] amaro, such as China-China, Nonino, or Montenegro

2 dashes Angostura bitters

Pinch flaky sea salt

4 ounces [120 ml] dry sparkling wine

1 or 2 very thin lemon or orange wheels, if desired

The Marseillan

Pastis is perhaps most at home in Marseille, where I've spent many a happy, sweaty, summer afternoon among the ranks of pétanque-playing octogenarians, café regulars, and salt-licked tourists nursing a pastis. When I'm not feeling the traditional measure of licorice-forward liquor lengthened with chilled water, I make this cocktail, which packs a little more punch and some welcome acid.

For 1

In a cocktail shaker, add the gin, lime juice, mint-lime syrup, and pastis. Strain into an ice-filled lowball glass and top with the chilled water.

1½ ounces [45 ml] gin

¾ ounce [22.5 ml] fresh lime juice

¾ ounce [22.5 ml] Mint-Lime Syrup (recipe follows)

½ ounce [15 ml] pastis

2 ounces [60 ml] chilled still mineral water

note on pastis | While Pernod (notes of star anise and fennel) and Ricard (licorice-forward) remain the best-known bottles on the market, I prefer to seek out herbal, nuanced, less-assertive Henri Bardouin, made an hour's drive north of Marseille in Forcalquier, or Argalà, which is made in the Italian village of Roccavione. If you're looking for a bottle to take home from a holiday in le sud, look for Pastis Millésimé Château des Creissauds or Pastis de la Plaine.

Mint-Lime Syrup

Makes 1¼ cups [300 ml]

Combine the fresh mint, lime zest, sugar, and salt in a small pot and muddle everything together. Cover and set aside at room temperature for at least 1 hour and up to 24 hours.

Add 1 cup [240 ml] of water to the pot and set over medium heat. Bring to a simmer, stirring to dissolve the sugar, then remove from the heat. Juice the zested limes and stir in the juice. Set aside to cool completely, then strain through a fine-mesh sieve, discarding the solids, and store, covered, in the refrigerator for up to 1 month.

1 large bunch fresh mint

2 limes, zested

1¼ cups [250 g] granulated sugar

1 teaspoon flaky salt

Citron Pressé, My Way

The first time I ordered a citron pressé in the south of France, I was handed a glass with an ounce or two of lemon juice alongside a bowl of sugar and a carafe of water to mix to my liking. In theory, how lovely! Choosing your own balance of acid to sweet! In practice, the sugar doesn't fully dissolve, and you end up paying upwards of 7€ for, yeah, lemon juice and water. Sometimes, though not always, if you order citronnade, you'll get it mixed and sweetened—though *then* I always wish I *could* adjust it to my taste. Here it is, the way it maybe ought to be.

1 to 2 ounces [30 to 60 ml] Citron Shrub (recipe follows)

3 to 6 ounces [90 to 180 ml] sparkling or still water, chilled

For 1

In a Collins glass, add the citron shrub to your liking. Top with chilled water and stir gently to combine. Serve over ice or not.

Citron Shrub

Makes just over 2 cups [480 ml]

Peel the lemons and place the citrus peels in a medium bowl or a large jar. Add the sugar and salt and use a muddler (or the end of a rolling pin) to muddle the mixture together, working the sugar mixture into the peels until the peels begin to express their oils and start to turn slightly translucent. Cover the bowl and set aside at room temperature for at least 6 hours or, if you have time, up to 24 hours.

Juice the lemons (you should have about 1¼ cups [300 ml] of juice) and add the juice to the muddled mixture; stir or cover and shake the jar until the sugar and salt dissolve. Strain through a fine-mesh sieve, pressing on the solids, and store, covered, in the refrigerator for up to 1 month.

6 large lemons

1¼ cups [250 g] granulated sugar

1 teaspoon flaky sea salt

Martini Provençal

A martini provençal is the drink I would serve to M.F.K. and Julia and Judith and Simone around the fire or on the terrace or in the garden at La Pitchoune if I could just find that tear in space-time. In this timeline, I've offered it to people I've had the good luck to love, from Arles to Ménerbes to Plascassier to Paris to New York to California.

For 1

In a mixing glass or shaker filled with ice, combine the vermouth, gin, sherry, and olive brine. Stir with a cocktail stirrer for 15 seconds, until the cocktail is very cold. Strain into a chilled Nick and Nora or an ice-filled lowball glass. Hold the lemon peel by its long edges, skin facing down into the glass. Pinch the peel to express the citrus oils into the glass, then discard the lemon peel. Serve the olives on the side, for the drinker to add or eat—or both—as they like.

1 ounce [30 ml] dry vermouth

1 ounce [30 ml] dry gin

½ ounce [15 ml] fino sherry

¼ ounce [7.5 ml] green olive brine, preferably Lucques or Castelvetrano

1 lemon peel

Green olives, preferably Lucques or Castelvetrano

Sans Fin

Make a round of sans fin now, continue drinking it...
forever? It's a spirited loop made possible by the practice of
keeping your bottled (or jarred) cocktail in the fridge and
each time you empty it, by one drink or six, topping off the
batch. The drink's 1:1 ratio makes an endless refresh easy
for even the least math-minded among us: For each drink
poured, add one ounce each of rye, cognac, vermouth,
and red bitter liqueur plus 1 teaspoon (⅙ ounce) of pastis
back into the bottle. The all-booze formula that allows for
this strategy crafts a strong, bitter-leaning drink—think the
Boulevardier meets Sazerac by way of Marseille. But if you
let the mix sit in the bottle a week or four before drinking,
say while you're on vacation or taking time off from
drinking, the spirits will soften in the bottle and the texture
of the drink will thicken slightly. Once you pour a glass or
two and refresh with fresh spirits, the sharper flavors and
textures will intertwine with those that have tempered with
time, gradually shifting sans fin into a drink that is distinct
to your house, apéro perpetually at the ready.

Makes 6 to 8 drinks, to start

Combine the rye, cognac, vermouth, red bitter, and pastis
in a spouted measuring cup or pitcher. Pour the cocktail
blend into a 750 ml bottle or jar, using a funnel if needed.

When ready to serve a drink, pour 3 to 4 ounces [90 to
120 ml] of the sans fin into an ice-filled lowball glass. Hold
a lemon peel by its long edges, skin facing down into the
glass. Pinch the peel to express the citrus oils into the glass,
then discard the lemon peel and serve.

note | I've been known to use Lillet Blanc in place of the
blanc vermouth and red vermouth when I'm out of blanc.
Also, bourbon when I'm out of rye, brandy when I'm out
of cognac. All to say: sans fin can and should be adapted to
your bar and your tastes.

6 ounces [180 ml] rye

6 ounces [180 ml] cognac

6 ounces [180 ml] blanc
vermouth

6 ounces [180 ml] red
bitter, such as Campari or
Cappelletti

1 ounce [30 ml] pastis

Lemon peels, for serving

Vin d'Orange

I'm mostly loath to make my own booze at home; my bar is already overflowing with bottles by others doing it very well. Vin d'orange is different. The Provençal apéritif is optimal when made by oneself, in batches just large enough to share here and there. Make it when bitter Seville oranges come into the market (end of December through mid-February in the northern hemisphere) and your vin d'orange will be ready by early spring. Don't drink it yet. Give it time, actively forgotten in the back of the refrigerator, finally pulling it out to serve chilled over ice all summer long. Or wait longer still and toast the year-end holidays with the peak fruits of labor past, starting the cycle again when the bottles run dry, another round for your future self.

Makes about 7 cups [1.7 L]

In a large sealable jar or container, add the rosé, eau de vie, and sugar. Gently stir to dissolve the sugar. Halve the oranges and cut each half into quarters or halves depending on the size of the oranges. Add the citrus wedges to the jar, then cover and store in the refrigerator or a cool, dark place for 30 days, stirring gently every few days (be careful not to stir too vigorously as extra juice from the citrus wedges makes the final product cloudy).

At 30 days, taste the vin d'orange. It should taste distinctly orange in flavor with a slight bitter edge. It may need a little more sugar and/or it may need to sit longer, up to 40 days total. When the vin d'orange is to your taste, strain through a double layer of cheesecloth into clean bottles or jars, discarding any sediment at the bottom of the container. Stored in tightly sealed containers, vin d'orange will keep in the refrigerator for up to 1 year. Serve chilled, over ice, or in a Vd'O (recipe follows).

note | If you can't find Seville oranges, use navel oranges plus 1 lemon (if you have them, throw a few halved kumquats in there too). For wine, use a dry rosé—Provençal if you can find it—or use a dry white wine. Some people add 1 vanilla bean, split and scraped; add it too, if you like.

Two 750 ml bottles dry rosé wine

1 cup [240 ml] eau de vie or vodka

⅔ cup [130 g] granulated sugar

1 pound [455 g] Seville oranges (4 to 6 oranges), rinsed well

Vd'O

When I have spare vin d'orange in the house and also want a cocktail, I make this.

For 1

In a mixing glass or shaker filled with ice, combine the vin d'orange, cognac, and orange liqueur. Stir with a cocktail stirrer for 15 seconds, until the cocktail is very cold. Strain into an ice-filled lowball glass, then top with the soda water. Add the orange wheel and serve.

note | If you don't have vin d'orange, use 2½ ounces [80 ml] Lillet Blanc or Lillet Rosé.

2½ ounces [80 ml] Vin d'Orange (facing page)

1 ounce [30 ml] cognac or brandy

½ ounce [15 ml] orange liqueur, such as Grand Marnier or Cointreau

2 ounces [60 ml] soda water

1 orange wheel

A LOT OF ROSÉ, SURE,

BUT NOT ONLY ROSÉ

Rosé is big business in Provence, a product of targeted marketing, geological position, climate, and three thousand hours of annual sun. It spans faintly pink and dry to tomato red and juicy to edging purple and lush. Some of it is excellent, some of it is very much not. To drink the good stuff, look to the producers who put in the time and love and—if you're like me and lean toward natural winemaking methods—don't touch the wine too much, by which I mean they add little to no sulfur and use grapes grown without pesticides or added sugars. Do your best to avoid rosé (any wine, really) that is made cheaply and meant to be sold quickly. And though marketing campaigns would have you think otherwise, rosé is not solely a summer juice; if you needed permission to give rosé a place at the table in every season, here it is.

There is also excellent wine that is not rosé in Provence.

Here are a few producers making very good stuff of all styles (rosé, pétillant, white, macerated, red) I love right now in Provence-Alpes-Côte d'Azur. It's not an exhaustive list and favors the natural and the low-intervention. Many bottles made by the names here are drinkable now, but maybe also set aside a bottle or two for your future self. If you can't find these bottles where you do your wine shopping, don't fret—first ask if they're able to bring any of them in and then ask for similar options.

Domaine Laura Aillaud | Laura Aillaud

Domaine des Passages | Marie Bélié

Les Maoù | Vincent + Aurélie Garreta

La Baladeuse | Fanny Daher

Clos des Mourres | Ingrid + Jean-Philippe Bouchet

Domaine Hauvette | Dominique Hauvette

Clos du Tilleul | Léa + Mathieu Malbec

Domaine Le Bars | Gwennaëlle Le Bars

Domaine Hélène Bleuzen | Hélène Bleuzen

Domaine Milan | Henri + Théophile Milan

Domaine Alloïs | Busi family

Val de Combrès | Valentin Létoquart

Domaine de Tara | Michèle + Patrick Folléa

Clos Sainte Magdeleine | Jonathan Sack

Domaine Les Terres Promises | Jean-Christophe Comor

Domaine Tempier | Peyraud Family + Daniel Ravier

Château Sainte Anne | Françoise + Jean-Baptiste Dutheil

Fondugues-Pradugues | Stephen Roberts

Les Tuiles Bleues | Céline Laforest

La Cabrery | Ferme Collective Longo Maï

Domaine du Petit Bonhomme | Fabien Chanavas

Campagne Sarrière | Ludovic Blairon

Cadavre Exquis | Marc + Shirine Salerno

Le Temps des Rêveurs | Jérôme Maillot

Kaya Tasman | Kaya Tasman

Clos de Trias | Even Bakke

Myrko Tépus | Myrko Tépus

Marianne Conan | Marianne Conan

La Réaltière | Sylvia + Pierre Michelland

Château Fontvert | Monod family

Château Revelette | Peter + Sandra Fischer

Domaine de la Combe au Mas | Marie-Sophie Jullien + Thomas Ayoun

Château Landra | Cécile + Frédéric Renoux

La Maison dans les Vignes | Julien Besson

La Ferme Viticole | Bastien Boutareaud

Figuière | Magali, Delphine + François Combard

Domaine de Sulauze | Karina + Guillaume Lefèvre

Terre Inconnue | Robert Creus

Château Bas | Philippe Pouchin

Domaine de l'Or Vert | Clément Jeannoutot + Aurélien Le Tellier

La Caillasse | Mélanie, Clément, Simon + Arthur

Les Champs Délicieux | Alexandre Dalet

Domaine de la Mongestine | Maxime Gamard, Céline + Harry Gozlan

Domaine de la Tour du Bon | Agnès Hocquard-Henry

Castell-Reynoard | Julien Castell

Domaine Terres d'Esclans | Agathe Chaussée + Fabrice Raymond

Clos des B | Gwendolyn Berger

Clos Saint-Joseph | Constance Malangé + Roch Sassi

Domaine de Vinceline | Vincent + Céline Dauby

Domaine des Claus | Léa Givet + Julien Bertaina

TO START

SNACKING

OPPOSITE:
Olives, Extra Spicy   **47**

Olives, Extra Spicy

Olives at a marché in Provence are in a class unto themselves. Jeweled piles, glistening in brine, bedecked with garlic or herbs, dénoyautées (pitted) or cassées (broken). Some are a mix of many types, others unilateral shrines to the crisp, green, torpedo-shaped Picholine; the tender, nutty, sweet Lucques; the jet-black, dry-cured, wrinkled, and meaty Nyon, the tiny, delicate, slightly sweet, slightly bitter Olive de Nice.

These, made with spicy, aromatic harissa, are my at-home ode to one of my personal market favorites: olives épicées.

Serves 6 | Makes about 3 cups [480 g]

In a medium saucepan over medium heat, combine the oil, garlic, lemon slices, and bay leaves. Cook, stirring occasionally, until the garlic is sizzling and golden, 5 to 8 minutes. Remove from the heat and stir in the harissa, vinegar, and basil. Set aside to cool for 30 minutes, then pour the oil mixture over the olives. Let sit at room temperature for at least 1 hour.

note | Olives can be marinated and kept chilled in an airtight container in the refrigerator up to 2 weeks ahead. Bring to room temperature before serving.

¾ cup [180 ml] extra-virgin olive oil

6 large garlic cloves, lightly crushed

1 small lemon, quartered, thinly sliced

2 bay leaves

2 tablespoons harissa

2 tablespoons sherry or red wine vinegar

4 sprigs fresh basil

1 pound [455 g] mixed olives

The -ades

Perhaps the most well-known in the legion of Provençal spreads, **tapenade** is made by pounding together olives, garlic, anchovies, capers, and olive oil in a large mortar. Leave out the anchovies and capers and you've made **olivade**. **Anchoïade** should be made garlicky and pungent with only the best anchovies. **Poivronade** relies on a combination of peppers and garlic, and **poischichade** on chickpeas, garlic, and lemon—both bound with a generous pour of olive oil. **Tomatade**, a personal and lesser-known favorite, is a thick purée of sweet, sun-dried tomatoes, toasted pine nuts, and, again, garlic. Make any of the -ades whenever and set out for apéro with crunchy vegetables or crusty bread. They will last, stored in separate airtight containers in the refrigerator, for 5 to 7 days.

Tapenade Noire ou Verte

Serves 4 to 6 | Makes about ¾ cup

2 small garlic cloves, coarsely chopped

3 anchovies, roughly chopped

2 tablespoons salted capers, rinsed, drained, and roughly chopped

¾ cup [105 g] pitted black olives (such as Niçoise or Kalamata) or green olives (such as Picholine or Lucques), roughly chopped

¼ cup [60 ml] extra-virgin olive oil

Freshly ground black pepper

If you are making the tapenade with a mortar and pestle: Place the garlic in a mortar and grind until a rough paste forms. Add the anchovies and capers and pound them, scraping the sides of the mortar often, until they are smashed into a mostly smooth paste. Add the olives and pound into a slightly chunky paste. Slowly add the oil, 1 tablespoon at a time, smashing until it's all combined. Season with pepper.

If you are making the tapenade with a food processor: Place the garlic in the bowl of a food processor and pulse until finely chopped. Add the anchovies and capers and pulse, scraping the sides of the food processor often, until they are finely ground. Add the olives and pulse until a slightly chunky paste forms. With the food processor running, slowly pour in the oil until it's all combined. Season with pepper.

Olivade Noire ou Verte

Serves 4 to 6 | Makes about ¾ cup

2 small garlic cloves, coarsely chopped

1¼ cups [175 g] pitted black olives (such as Niçoise or Kalamata) or green olives (such as Picholine or Lucques)

¼ cup [60 ml] extra-virgin olive oil

If you are making the olivade with a mortar and pestle: Place the garlic in a mortar and grind until a rough paste forms. Add the olives and pound them, scraping the sides of the mortar often, until they are smashed into a slightly chunky, thick paste. Slowly add the oil, 1 tablespoon at a time, smashing until it's all combined.

If you are making the olivade with a food processor: Place the garlic in the bowl of a food processor and pulse until finely chopped. Add the olives and pulse, scraping the sides of the food processor often, until a slightly chunky, thick paste forms. With the food processor running, slowly pour in the oil until it's all combined.

Anchoïade

Serves 4 to 6 | Makes a scant ⅔ cup

2 garlic cloves, coarsely chopped

1 tablespoon finely chopped fresh flat-leaf parsley

20 anchovy fillets, coarsely chopped

1 teaspoon red wine vinegar or fresh lemon juice

¼ cup [60 ml] extra-virgin olive oil

Freshly ground black pepper

If you are making the anchoïade with a mortar and pestle: Place the garlic and parsley in a mortar and grind until a rough paste forms. Add the anchovies and pound them, scraping the sides of the mortar often, until they are smashed into a mostly smooth paste. Stir in the vinegar, then slowly add the oil, 1 tablespoon at a time, smashing until it's all combined. Season with pepper.

If you are making the anchoïade with a food processor: Place the garlic in the bowl of a food processor and pulse until finely chopped. Add the parsley and anchovies and pulse, scraping the sides of the food processor often, until they are finely ground. Add the vinegar and pulse just to mix. With the food processor running, slowly pour in the oil until it's all combined. Season with pepper.

Poivronade

Serves 4 to 6 | Makes about 1¼ cups

Preheat the oven to 400°F [200°C]. Place the bell peppers on a baking sheet and drizzle with 1 tablespoon of the olive oil. Use your hands to rub the oil all over, then roast for 25 minutes. Use tongs to turn the peppers. Continue roasting until they are charred all over, 15 to 20 minutes more. Remove from the oven and transfer the peppers to a bowl, cover the bowl with a plate, and set aside to cool.

Once cooled, remove and discard the skins, seeds, and stems from the peppers. Transfer the peppers to a food processor along with the garlic and remaining 2 tablespoons of olive oil. Blend until a coarse purée forms. Stir in the vinegar and season with salt.

2 medium red bell peppers

3 tablespoons extra-virgin olive oil

1 garlic clove, grated on a Microplane

2 teaspoons red wine vinegar

Fine sea salt

Poischichade

Serves 4 to 6 | Makes about 1¼ cups

Add the chickpeas, 2 tablespoons of the reserved aquafaba, the garlic, lemon juice, and the preserved lemon and cumin (if using) to the bowl of a food processor and pulse until roughly chopped. Pulse again, scraping the sides of the food processor often, until a slightly chunky, thick paste forms. With the food processor running, slowly pour in the oil until it's all combined. Add the remaining aquafaba to thin the poischichade as needed, blending until a smooth purée forms. Season with salt.

One 14-ounce [400 g] can chickpeas, drained and ¼ cup [60 ml] aquafaba (liquid) reserved

1 garlic clove, grated on a Microplane

1 lemon, juiced

1 tablespoon finely chopped Preserved (Meyer) Lemons (page 81), if desired

¼ teaspoon cumin, if desired

¼ cup [60 ml] extra virgin olive oil

Fine sea salt

Tomatade

Serves 4 to 6 | Makes about 1 cup

Place the garlic in the bowl of a food processor and pulse until finely chopped. Add the pine nuts and pulse until finely chopped. Add the tomatoes and basil and pulse, scraping the sides of the food processor often, until a slightly chunky, thick purée forms. With the food processor running, slowly pour in the oil until it's all combined. Season with salt and pepper.

1 garlic clove, coarsely chopped

¼ cup [30 g] pine nuts, toasted, cooled, and coarsely chopped

1 cup [150 g] sun-dried tomatoes packed in oil, coarsely chopped

10 basil leaves

¼ cup [60 ml] extra-virgin olive oil

Fine sea salt

Freshly ground black pepper

Caviar d'Aubergines

Cavaillon, a small town between Avignon and Aix-en-Provence, is quite dear to me, and not only because it's home to a certain melon (see page 225). It is mostly about the melon, but it's also where, during a holiday with friends, I perfected the art of the swim-up apéro. The setup is fairly self-explanatory, but if you have the luck to be by a pool—any pool, this summer or anytime—make this smoky eggplant dip (pictured on page 54). Once apéro hour approaches, arrange the dip and plenty of chips and/or crunchy vegetables just close enough to the pool's edge. Add Piscines (page 24) or Citron Pressé, My Way (page 31)—in shatterproof glasses, mind. You know what happens next.

Serves 6 | Makes about 1½ cups

Preheat the oven to 400°F [200°C].

Use a sharp knife to cut small slits in the flesh of each eggplant and place them whole on a baking sheet. Bake until the eggplants are very tender, 45 minutes to 1 hour. Set aside to cool.

Slice the eggplants in half lengthwise. Scoop out the flesh, discarding the skin and stalks, and transfer to the bowl of a food processor. Add the garlic and pulse to combine into a thick paste. With the motor running, slowly pour in the olive oil, processing until the mixture becomes a smooth paste. Add the basil and parsley and pulse a few more times to combine. Stir in the lemon juice and season generously with smoked salt and pepper. Serve immediately or store in an airtight container for up to 3 days.

note | I don't often have ready access to a gas stove or an outdoor grill to cook my eggplants directly on the flame until the skin is blackened and the eggplants are very soft. If you do, do so, by all means. If you don't, smoked salt imparts a goût fumé.

2 large eggplants
(2 to 2½ pounds
[910 g to 1.2 kg] total)

1 garlic clove, grated on a Microplane

½ cup [120 ml] extra-virgin olive oil

3 tablespoons finely chopped fresh basil

3 tablespoons finely chopped fresh flat-leaf parsley

1 lemon, juiced

Smoked salt or standard fine sea salt

Freshly ground black pepper

Chips + Pist-ail

Should you spot me at the marché in Provence, bobbing and weaving through the crowd, I'm likely looking for pist-ail. The first time I came across the light green, boring-looking spread (boring, at least, relative to the nearby olives and tapenades and sun-dried tomatoes) was at the massive, wonderful Saturday marche in Arles. Later that day, I spooned a bit of the creamy, potent, herbal spread into a small bowl and opened a bag of chips—a not-atypical pre-apéro apéro for one. I spooned a little more. By the time friends arrived for the apéro apéro, there was little left and I was hooked.

Serves 4 to 6 | Makes about ¾ cup

In the bowl of a food processor, add the steamed garlic, lemon juice, and salt. Pulse until the mixture forms a paste, scraping down the sides of the bowl as necessary. With the motor running, very slowly pour in the olive oil, starting drop by drop, processing until the mixture becomes a thick, smooth paste. Add the basil leaves and pulse, scraping the sides of the food processor often, until fully combined. With the motor running, slowly drizzle in the ice water until a smooth, creamy spread forms. Serve with potato chips. The pist-ail will keep, stored in an airtight container in the refrigerator, for up to 3 days.

note | To steam garlic, start by using fresh garlic, looking for firm, tight heads without signs of bruising or sprouting. Peel the cloves and place in a steamer insert. Add enough water to a pan to come about 1½ to 2 inches [4 to 5 cm] up the sides of the pan and bring to a boil. Lower the heat, cover, and steam until the garlic is very soft, about 20 minutes.

½ cup [80 g] peeled garlic cloves (16 to 18 garlic cloves), steamed (see Note)

1 tablespoon fresh lemon juice

½ teaspoon fine sea salt

⅓ cup [80 ml] extra-virgin olive oil

2 cups [50 g] tightly packed fresh basil leaves, stems discarded

2 tablespoons ice water

Potato chips, for serving

Crudité + Beurre Pommade

Olive oil may be the queen of hearts in Provence, but folks, we're still in France here, and butter reigns eternal. Go next level by erecting a tower of it laced with lemon zest and sprinkled with garlicky, anchovy-y bread crumbs at your next apéro/party.

Serves a crowd

Set a small skillet over medium heat and add 2 tablespoons of the butter. Once the butter is melted, add the garlic and anchovies and cook, stirring, until toasted and fragrant, about 1 minute. Stir in the bread crumbs and season with salt, pepper, and red pepper flakes (if using). Cook, stirring frequently, until the bread crumbs are toasted, 3 to 5 minutes.

In a bowl with a spatula or very clean hands, combine the remaining butter and the lemon zest; mix until smooth and creamy. Season with salt, then transfer to a serving plate, using your hands or the spatula to form the butter into a tall mound. Sprinkle the bread crumb mixture over the beurre pommade and serve with crudités and crusty bread. Should you have leftover beurre pommade, transfer to an airtight container and store in the refrigerator for up to 5 days. It'll be less dramatic than the tower and the bread crumbs may lose some of their crunch, but it'll be no less delicious.

1 pound [455 g] unsalted European butter, at room temperature

1 large garlic clove, finely chopped or grated on a Microplane

2 anchovies, finely chopped

½ cup [70 g] fine bread crumbs

Flaky sea salt

Freshly ground black pepper

Red pepper flakes, if desired

1 lemon, zested

Radishes and other crudités, for serving

Crusty bread, for serving

Pink Peppercorn Marinated Chèvre

Mornings in Antibes—a charming seaside peninsula between Cannes and Nice—revolve around the daily covered market on Cours Masséna. Start at the coffee shop and end at the boulangerie, each tucked a few winding, narrow, relentlessly charming streets away from the marché. If the cheese stall happens to have tomette à l'huile—a round of bright white chèvre in olive oil, topped with dried herbs and a shock of pink peppercorns—get that, or ask for the freshest chèvre they have and make it yourself. Add a baguette, and there you have your afternoon.

Makes one 3-inch [7.5 cm] round

Add 1 tablespoon of the olive oil to the bottom of a clean, sterilized wide-mouthed jar or a bowl just big enough to fit the cheese. Add the cheese to the jar and top with peppercorns and herbes de Provence. Pour the remaining olive oil over the top (it should cover the cheese completely; if it doesn't, add more to cover). Cover the jar and marinate for 2 hours at room temperature or overnight in the refrigerator. The marinated chèvre can be kept in the refrigerator for up to 1 week.

note | Serve the cheese in the oil, and use a baguette to make sure none of it gets left behind.

note | Herbes de Provence is an all-purpose, aromatic dried herb mix made of rosemary, thyme, oregano, and savory (and sometimes also basil, marjoram, fennel, sage, and lavender)—all plants that grow in happy abundance across Provence-Alpes-Côte d'Azur. To make your own, hang bundles of whatever fresh herbs you want to include in your herbes de Provence in a dry corner of the house. Once the herbs are very dry, pull them from their stems, crush them, and combine in equal portions. Store in a jar for up to 6 months, but use before then.

¼ cup [60 ml] extra-virgin olive oil, plus more if needed

6 ounces [170 g] fresh chèvre, either one 3-inch [7.5 cm] round or a small log cut into rounds

1 tablespoon whole pink peppercorns

1 teaspoon dried herbes de Provence (see Note)

Radishes + Radish Leaf Pesto

I started making this pesto in a rental kitchen in Menton, inspired loosely by a morning run across the French-Italian border to the market in Ventimiglia in which I got so distracted by the fiore sardo (cheese!), the spianata piccante (Calabrian salami!), and the purple-leaved carciofi (artichokes!) that I forgot to buy basil. For my pesto. Now, rather than making it work with extra radish leaves, I buy radishes to make this pesto. Serve it up with the good butter and let everyone assemble their ideal bite.

Serves 6 | Makes 1½ cup [360 ml]

In a blender or food processor, add the radish leaves, mint leaves, and garlic. Pulse to coarsely combine. With the mixer running, add the oil in a steady stream, blending until the pesto is smooth. Add the lemon zest and juice and pulse to combine. Stir in the Parmigiano-Reggiano and season with salt and pepper. Serve with cleaned, chilled, and halved radishes.

Radish leaf pesto can be made up to 3 days in advance and stored, covered with additional olive oil drizzled over the top, in the refrigerator.

1 large bunch radishes, leaves and vegetables separated, leaves picked and cleaned (about 3 tightly packed cups [100 g] leaves)

1 large bunch fresh mint, leaves cleaned and picked, stems discarded (about 1½ packed cup [30 g])

1 small garlic clove, grated on a Microplane

¾ cup [180 ml] extra-virgin olive oil

1 lemon, zested and juiced

1 cup [40 g] finely grated Parmigiano-Reggiano

Fine sea salt

Freshly ground black pepper

Zucchini Blossoms

If there are beignets de fleurs de courgettes (fried zucchini blossoms) on a menu, expect me to order them. The best I've had were at La Merenda, a tiny, hallowed, twelve-seat temple to Niçoise cooking a few blocks from the Cours Saleya market in Nice. Their fried blossoms are crisp and nearly weightless, sprinkled with pops of sea salt. Whenever I bring a bouquet of blossoms home, I channel that memory. While they serve their fleurs unadulterated, I often pair mine with an anchovy-laced aïoli (see page 161).

Serves 6 to 8

Line a baking sheet with paper towels and set aside.

Combine the flour and fine sea salt in a medium bowl and gradually whisk in the club soda until the batter is nearly smooth.

In a wide, deep saucepan, add enough oil to come about ½ inch [12 mm] up the sides of the pan. Place over medium-high heat. Once the oil is hot, add the lemon slices in a single layer, working in batches if needed to avoid crowding the pan. Cook until the edges of the lemon slices are beginning to caramelize, 5 to 6 minutes, then flip the lemons and cook 1 to 2 minutes more. Transfer to the paper towel–lined sheet and sprinkle with flaky sea salt.

Once all the lemons are fried, working one blossom at a time, gently twist the end of the blossoms to close and dredge the blossoms in the batter. Gently shake off any excess and place the blossoms in the oil without crowding the pan. Cook the blossoms in batches until the edges become golden, about 1 minute, then gently rotate each blossom in the oil and continue to fry until golden on the second side, 30 seconds more. Rotate once more to ensure the entire blossom is golden. Cook for 30 seconds more, then transfer to the prepared baking sheet and sprinkle with flaky sea salt. Immediately transfer the blossoms and fried lemons to a warm platter and serve in hot batches with fresh lemon wedges, repeating until everything is fried.

⅓ cup plus 2 tablespoons [65 g] all-purpose flour

1 teaspoon fine sea salt

½ cup [120 ml] club soda or light beer, cold

Vegetable or olive oil, for frying

1 medium lemon, thinly sliced and seeds removed

Flaky sea salt

16 zucchini blossoms, stems and stamens removed

Lemon wedges, for serving

Sardines + Piment d'Espelette

While sick with long COVID, I spent the month of October in La Ciotat, a port city on the Mediterranean near Bandol, attempting to harness the restorative powers of the sea. One day, a friend drove in to meet me for a picnic and, my recovery pantry sparse, I grabbed a tin of sardines to contribute. In a story too long for this headnote, that tin of sardines directly led to meeting the woman who is now my wife. TL;DR: tinned fish > flowers.

Serves 6

Open the sardine tins. Top with lemon zest and piment d'Espelette. Sprinkle with salt and serve with bread, butter, lemon quarters, and more salt and piment d'Espelette.

note | Piment d'Espelette is a lightly spiced chile from France's Basque country. I highly recommend seeking it out at specialty shops or online and then putting it on most things—it's very special—but hot paprika can be substituted here if necessary.

Two 5-ounce [140 g] tins sardines packed in oil

1 lemon, zested and quartered

1 teaspoon piment d'Espelette, plus more for serving

Flaky sea salt

Crusty bread, for serving

Salted European butter, for serving

Tarte Soleil

I spotted the lone square of ripe, thinly sliced tomatoes shingled over puff pastry and blanketed in herbes de Provence tucked between a pile of croissants and pains au chocolat at a bakery in Antibes. I snagged it. A few months later, something similar during a trip to Marseille: pâte feuilletée covered edge-to-edge with a rainbow of heirlooms, a swipe of mustard hidden underneath. Then, this recipe.

Serves 6 to 8

Line a large baking sheet with paper towels. Arrange the sliced tomatoes in a single layer and season with salt on both sides. Let sit for 30 minutes, then pat the tops of the tomatoes dry with paper towels.

Preheat the oven to 400°F [200°C]. Line a baking sheet with parchment paper.

In a small bowl, stir together the crème fraîche, mustard, and 2 teaspoons of the herbes de Provence. Season with salt and pepper. Transfer the puff pastry to a lightly floured surface and roll into a 15-by-10-inch [38 by 25 cm] rectangle (the dough should be about ⅛ inch [4 mm] thick).

Transfer the puff pastry to the prepared baking sheet and use a fork to prick it all over. Use an offset spatula to spread the crème fraîche mixture in an even layer over the puff pastry, leaving about ¼-inch [6 mm] border. Layer the tomato slices on top of the crème fraîche, overlapping them slightly. Sprinkle with the remaining 1 teaspoon of herbes de Provence and black pepper.

Bake, rotating the sheet halfway through, until the puff pastry is deeply golden, about 40 minutes. Serve warm or at room temperature. Tarte soleil is best eaten the day it is made.

4 pounds [1.8 kg] medium heirloom tomatoes (8 to 10 total), halved lengthwise and sliced into ⅛-inch [4 mm] thick half moons

Flaky sea salt

¼ cup [60 g] crème fraîche

2 tablespoons grainy mustard

3 teaspoons herbes de Provence (see Note, page 59)

Freshly ground black pepper

All-purpose flour, for dusting

One 14-ounce [400 g] package all-butter puff pastry

Pickled Things + Saucisson

Whenever I pop into one of my favorite fromageries, Maison Moga, in L'Isle-sur-la-Sorgue, I load up on local Provençal cheeses, then repeat with their exceptional charcuterie. I ask them to slice my choice cured meat into very, very thin rounds. When I get home, I directly top said rounds with a combination of quick pickles—soft-edged zucchini, piquant shallots, and crunchy radishes—but if all you find yourself with is a jar of cornichons or kosher dills, by all means. The key here, no matter the charcuterie, is to ask your Maison Moga equivalent (a.k.a. your butcher or cheesemonger or deli woman who has access to a commercial meat slicer) to slice it into very, very thin rounds. The contrast in textures, spice, and acidity are really it.

Serves 6 to 8

In a strainer, combine the zucchini and shallots and season with 1 teaspoon of the salt. Toss to coat, then set aside to drain for 2 hours, tossing again halfway through. Using a linen or paper towel, squeeze the excess moisture out and add the zucchini and shallots to a medium bowl or jar.

Add the radishes to a separate medium bowl or jar. In a third jar, combine the vinegar, sugar, red pepper flakes, and the remaining 1 teaspoon of salt. Cover and shake vigorously to dissolve the sugar and salt. Uncover and pour ¼ cup [60 ml] of the vinegar mixture over the radishes. Pour the remainder of the vinegar mixture over the zucchini and shallots and set aside for at least 30 minutes and up to 2 hours. The pickles can be made ahead and kept in the refrigerator for up to 5 days.

To serve, arrange the saucisson in a single overlapping layer on a serving platter. Top with the pickled zucchini, shallots, and radishes.

note | For the base layer, saucisson sec is my go-to, but soppressata, finocchiona, coppa, salami, or any other high-quality cured meat you like will work.

1 medium zucchini, very thinly sliced

3 shallots, very thinly sliced

2 teaspoons fine sea salt

12 radishes, cut into ½-inch [12 mm] pieces

⅔ cup [160 ml] red wine vinegar

2 tablespoons granulated sugar

1 teaspoon red pepper flakes

4 ounces [115 g] saucisson sec, very thinly sliced into rounds

Anchovy Choux

I first learned to make pâte à choux in pastry school in my early twenties, piping the thick, sticky dough into éclairs and profiteroles. Then, when I moved from New York to Paris, it was savory pâte à choux over and over by way of shiny, stretchy dough run through with a gratable cheese to make gougères. But it wasn't until I started spending time in Provence that I came to know anchovy choux. Quite the same versatile butter–flour–egg–water, but now laced with bits of salty, briny anchovies.

Makes 28 to 32 choux

Line two large baking sheets with parchment paper.

In a medium saucepan over medium-high heat, combine 1 cup [240 ml] of water, the butter, and fine sea salt. Heat until the butter is melted and the mixture is hot but not boiling.

Add the flour all at once, lower the heat to medium, and use a wooden spoon to stir constantly until the dough pulls away from the sides of the pan, a smooth ball forms, and the mixture starts to leave a film on the pan, 3 to 4 minutes.

Transfer the dough to the bowl of a stand mixer fitted with a paddle attachment. Mix on medium-low speed until the bowl no longer feels hot to the touch, then add the eggs, one at a time, making sure each is mixed in before adding the next. Once all the eggs are added, increase the speed to medium-high and beat for 15 minutes. Add the anchovies and pepper and mix just to combine.

Preheat the oven to 400°F [200°C].

Scoop heaping tablespoons of the dough onto the prepared baking sheets, spacing each spoonful about 1½ inches [4 cm] apart. Sprinkle with flaky sea salt and pepper. Place in the oven, immediately lower the temperature to 375°F [190°C], and bake until puffed and deeply golden brown, 20 to 25 minutes, rotating the pans halfway through. Serve warm or at room temperature.

note | The puffs can be shaped, frozen, and kept in an airtight container for up to 1 month, then baked off as needed (add a few minutes to the baking time).

6 tablespoons [85 g] unsalted European butter, diced

½ teaspoon fine sea salt

1 cup [140 g] all-purpose flour

4 large eggs, at room temperature

10 anchovy fillets, finely chopped

1 teaspoon freshly ground black pepper, plus more to finish

Flaky sea salt

Pissaladière

The best pissaladière I've had in this lifetime is a three-way tie between one eaten at a marché in Èze, another at a marché in Vence (after an equally memorable visit to La Chapelle Matisse), and a third at a small boulangerie in Antibes. Each was made with a yeasted dough and piled high with caramelized onions, anchovies, and cured olives. While in recent years I've happily eaten and made excellent pissaladières with a richer, thinner base of puff pastry, the heart wants what it wants, and I still prefer pissaladières that lean thicker, nearly-but-not-quite focaccia in their risen, airy crusts, made with enough olive oil to soak through the bag before you've left the marché or bakery.

Serves 8 | Makes one 9-inch [23 cm] round pissaladière

To make the dough: In a large bowl, whisk together the yeast, honey, and water. Let stand for 5 minutes (the mixture should be foamy), then whisk in 1 tablespoon of the oil. Add the flour and salt and stir with a wooden spoon until a sticky dough forms.

Rub the inside of another large bowl with 1 tablespoon of olive oil and transfer the dough to the bowl, rubbing the top of the dough with your oily hands. Cover with plastic wrap or reusable beeswax wrap and let rest overnight in the refrigerator. The dough should about double in size.

The next day, rub a 9-inch [23 cm] round baking pan evenly with 1 tablespoon of the olive oil. Transfer the dough to the pan and use your hands to gently stretch the dough to the edge of the pan. Cover with a cloth or towel and set aside until the dough is bubbly, light, and doubled again in size, 1 to 2 hours. While the dough rises, make the topping. CONTINUED

DOUGH

1 teaspoon active dry yeast

1 teaspoon honey

¾ cup [180 ml] warm water

5 tablespoons [80 ml] extra-virgin olive oil

1½ cups [210 g] all-purpose flour

¾ teaspoon fine sea salt

TOPPING

10 to 12 anchovies packed in oil

¼ cup [60 ml] extra-virgin olive oil

3 pounds [1.4 kg] white onions, thinly sliced

2 sprigs fresh thyme

Fine sea salt

¼ cup [35 g] Niçoise or other cured black olives

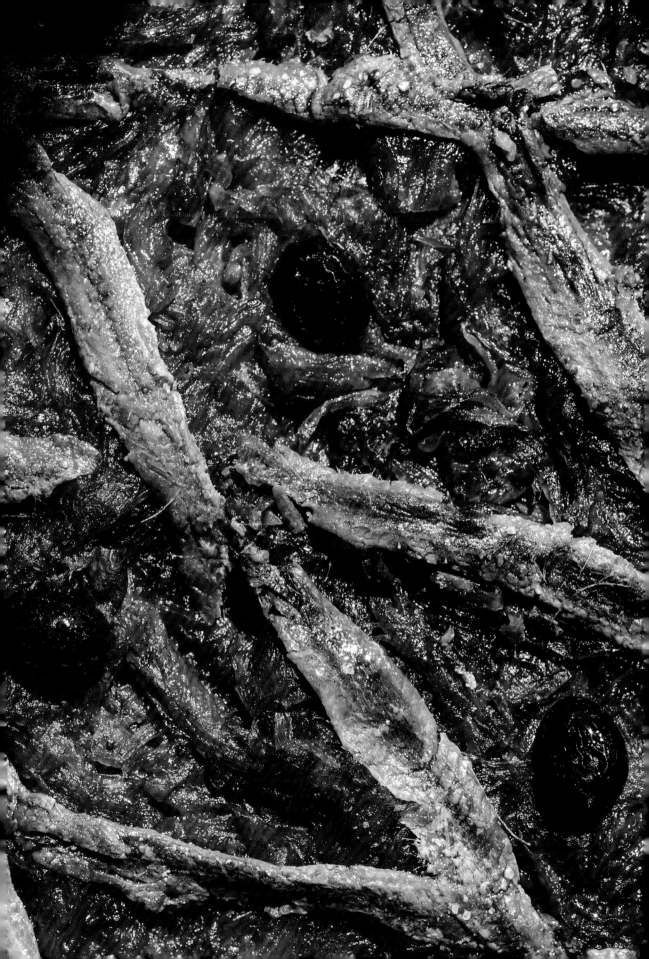

To make the topping: Finely chop 2 of the anchovies. Set a large skillet over medium heat and add the ¼ cup [60 ml] of olive oil. Once the oil is hot, add the onions and cook, stirring frequently, until the onions are tender and translucent, about 15 minutes. Add the chopped anchovies and thyme sprigs and season lightly with salt. Lower the heat to medium-low and continue to cook, stirring occasionally, until the onions are golden and soft, 35 to 45 minutes. Remove from the heat, remove and discard the thyme sprigs, and set aside to cool.

To bake: Arrange an oven rack near the bottom of the oven. If you have a baking stone, place it on the rack. Otherwise, invert a baking sheet and place it on the rack. Preheat the oven to 450°F [230°C].

Use your fingertips to press dimples in the dough and drizzle with the remaining 2 tablespoons of olive oil. Bake for 20 minutes; the dough should be puffed and lightly browned. Remove the pan from the oven and carefully spread the prepared onion mixture evenly over the top. Top with the 8 to 10 remaining anchovies and the olives. (I sometimes do this in a more traditional diamond pattern. You do you.) Lower the oven temperature to 400°F [200°C] and continue to bake until the onions are deeply golden brown, 10 to 15 minutes more. Let the pissaladiére cool in the pan. Serve warm or at room temperature.

Panisse

Up and down the coast of Provence-Alpes-Côte d'Azur, all manner of chickpea flour–based snacks are made on the daily and sold at restaurants, markets, streetside stands, and from the back of woodfire oven–carting bicycles. Crisp-edged panisses (pictured on page 77) are served for apéro in Marseille, the thick batter cut into sticks or rounds, fried to order, and served hot with rosé. Lines for socca spill into the streets of Nice, the thinner batter poured into wide, shallow copper pans and baked in wood-fired ovens, the resulting pancakes served with a generous dusting of black pepper. Cade Toulonnaise, made with socca's same batter poured in a thicker layer, is de rigueur in Toulon. They're all great, but if I had to choose one, it's panisse for me.

Serves 6 to 8 | Makes about 30 to 36 panisses

Line a 9-by-13-inch [23 by 33 cm] baking pan or quarter sheet pan with one long piece of parchment paper overhanging the long sides of the pan. Brush lightly with a little olive oil and set aside.

In a medium pot, add 4 cups [960 ml] of water, the olive oil, fine sea salt, and pepper. Bring to a simmer over medium-high heat, then gradually whisk in the chickpea flour until combined. Lower the heat to maintain a simmer and cook, whisking constantly, until the mixture thickens and starts to bubble, then switch to a wooden spoon and continue cooking, stirring continuously, until the mixture is very thick, smooth, and stiff, 10 to 15 minutes.

Immediately pour the mixture into the prepared pan and smooth the top (the batter should be about ¾ inch [2 cm] thick). Set aside to cool slightly at room temperature, then cover tightly with plastic wrap, pressing the wrap directly onto the surface, and refrigerate until firm, at least 3 hours and up to 2 days.

1 tablespoon extra-virgin olive oil, plus more for the pan

1 teaspoon fine sea salt

Freshly ground black pepper

2½ cups [300 g] fine chickpea flour

2 to 3 cups [480 to 720 ml] grapeseed oil, for frying

Flaky sea salt

Preserved Lemon Aïoli (recipe follows)

When you are ready to fry the panisses, remove the pan from the refrigerator and, grasping the edges of the parchment paper, transfer the chilled, firm rectangle of batter to a cutting board. Using a long, sharp knife, cut the batter into 3-by-1-inch [7.5 by 2.5 cm] pieces.

Line a large heatproof plate or baking sheet with paper towels and set aside.

In a large, high-sided skillet, add enough grapeseed oil to come about ½ inch [12 mm] up the sides of the pan. Heat over medium-high until shimmering, then add the panisse in batches, taking care not to crowd the pan. Cook until golden and crisp on all sides, flipping halfway through, 5 to 8 minutes total. Transfer to the prepared baking sheet, and season generously with flaky sea salt. Repeat with the remaining panisse, adding more oil as needed. Serve hot, alone, or with preserved lemon aïoli.

Preserved Lemon Aïoli

Makes about 1 cup [240 ml]

In a medium bowl, whisk together the egg yolks, mustard, and garlic. Whisking constantly, add the grapeseed oil drop by drop until the mixture thickens. Continuing to whisk constantly, pour in the olive oil in a slow, steady stream. Add the lemon juice in 1-teaspoon increments, whisking constantly. The aïoli mixture should be yellow and thick. Stir in the preserved lemon and transfer to a serving bowl. Aïoli will keep, stored in an airtight container in the refrigerator, for 1 day.

2 large egg yolks

1 teaspoon Dijon mustard

1 to 2 small garlic cloves, grated on a Microplane

¼ cup [60 ml] grapeseed or canola oil

½ cup [120 ml] extra-virgin olive oil

2 tablespoons fresh lemon juice

1 tablespoon finely chopped Preserved (Meyer) Lemons (page 81, or store bought)

Preserved (Meyer) Lemons

I use Meyer lemons here but if you can get your hands on Menton lemons (see page 229), by all means. If you can't get your hands on either, use standard lemons, looking for those with thinner skins.

Makes 4 preserved lemons

Cut the Meyer lemons into quarters lengthwise, leaving the bottom connected. Add 2 tablespoons of the salt to the bottom of a medium jar. Working one at a time over a small bowl, gently open each Meyer lemon and sprinkle generously with salt, covering the insides of the lemons well. Add 2 lemons to the jar, pressing down firmly to squeeze out most of their juice.

Sprinkle with 1 tablespoon of the salt and add the bay leaves (if using). Add the remaining 2 sliced and salted Meyer lemons, squeezing them into the jar and pressing on them to release the juices. Sprinkle with any remaining salt.

Juice the standard lemon into the jar, so the Meyer lemons are completely submerged. Cover and set aside at room temperature for 3 weeks, checking the lemons occasionally to ensure they are completely submerged (if they aren't, open and use a clean wooden spoon to pack them tightly into the jar). After 3 weeks, transfer the jar to the refrigerator. The preserved Meyer lemons will keep, tightly covered and refrigerated, for up to 1 year.

4 medium Meyer lemons

½ cup [80 g] kosher salt

2 fresh or dried bay leaves, if desired

1 or 2 standard lemons

Candied Walnuts

When I first tossed a few handfuls of walnuts with honey and herbes de Provence, it was to use up the leftover nuts from making Radicchio Salad with Poached Quince (page 213). Then I ate them. I ate them for apéro with a round of Piscines (page 24). Then with coffee as a travel snack during the surprisingly long train ride from Cannes back to Paris. Then with cognac after dinner because I am that bitch. When they were gone, I made them again and again.

Now you make them.

Makes 4 cups [480 g]

Preheat the oven to 325°F [165°C]. Line a baking sheet with parchment paper.

In a large bowl, add the walnuts, honey, olive oil, rosemary, herbes de Provence, salt, and cayenne (if using). Toss to coat, then spread the walnuts evenly in a single layer on the prepared baking sheet and place in the oven to cook, tossing occasionally, until toasted and fragrant, about 20 minutes. Remove from the oven and set aside to cool completely. Candied walnuts will keep, stored in a tightly sealed container at room temperature, for up to 2 weeks.

note | Swap in another nut or a mix of nuts for the walnuts, if you like.

note | If your honey isn't super fluid, warm it slightly in a small saucepan set over low heat just until warm and runny.

4 cups [480 g] walnut halves (see Note)

⅓ cup [115 g] honey, preferably lavender (see Note)

2 tablespoons extra-virgin olive oil

2 tablespoons finely chopped fresh rosemary

2 teaspoons herbes de Provence (see Note, page 59)

2 teaspoons flaky sea salt

Pinch cayenne pepper, if desired

Banon + Mushrooms

Forgive me if you're planning on making this recipe in the United States, as you likely won't be able to find Banon—the cheese is unpasteurized and aged under 30 days and thus illegal to import stateside by no fault of its own. So, use another strong goat cheese or even a round of ripe Camembert instead. BUT if and when you come to Provence (or elsewhere in France or Europe), you're going to want to find a round of Banon. It won't be hard. You can serve it as is. The AOP (appellation d'origine protégée) goat's milk cheese is made in Haute Provence, wrapped in chestnut leaves, and bound with raffia and has all its complex, velvety flavor contained within. But the act of tossing warm mushrooms on top further enhances the inherent savory, earthy notes, nudging its tender, spoonable texture toward flowing.

Serves 6

Two or three 3½ ounce [100 g] rounds Banon cheese, at room temperature

2 tablespoons extra-virgin olive oil

2 shallots, thinly sliced

12 ounces [340 g] mushrooms, such as chanterelle, trumpet, or cremini, cleaned and trimmed

2 sprigs fresh thyme

2 garlic cloves, finely chopped

¼ cup [60 ml] sweet wine, such as Muscat de Beaume-de-Venise or Sauternes (see Note)

Fine sea salt

Freshly ground black pepper

2 tablespoons unsalted European butter, at room temperature

Crusty bread, for serving

Partially unwrap the Banon and artfully arrange on a platter or plate.

In a large skillet over medium-high heat, heat the olive oil until hot. Add the shallots and cook, stirring, until tender, about 5 minutes. Add the mushrooms and thyme and stir to coat with the oil. Cook, stirring occasionally, until the mushrooms are lightly browned, about 5 minutes. Add the garlic and cook, stirring, for 1 minute more, then pour in the wine and cook until all the liquid has nearly evaporated, about 2 minutes more. Season with salt and pepper, then add the butter and cook until the butter is melted and the mushrooms are very tender, about 2 minutes more. Remove the pan from the heat and immediately spoon the hot mushrooms over the cheese rounds. Serve hot with bread.

note | If you don't have Muscat de Beaume-de-Venise or Sauternes, use blanc vermouth, Lillet, or a white wine you enjoy drinking. If you don't want to use alcohol at all, use 2 tablespoons water and 2 tablespoons apple cider vinegar.

SNACKING MATTERS

STORE-BOUGHT APÉRITIF SNACKS
(SOME FRENCH, SOME FRENCH-LEANING,
SOME NOT FRENCH AT ALL) TO KEEP ON HAND

———————

Barring the afternoon goûter of school children, it's true: Snacking between meals isn't really a thing in France. Unless, of course, you swap in the word *snack* for *apéro*. Pausing for a drink and small bite during l'heure de l'apéritif is sacred across France—and very much to me. Every recipe in the pages leading up to this essay are prime apéro material, but if you don't feel like following a recipe, even the tiniest, non-cooking bit (page 66), here are some of my favorite à la minute snacks. Some are very French, some French-leaning, others not French at all but no less worthy. Expand this list to your likes, your discoveries, your guests' delights.

This snack, by any other name, is still a snack.

Chips | salt + vinegar or ruffled, preferably

Popcorn | salty or sweet

Nuts | walnuts, almonds, pistachios, hazelnuts; shelled or in the shell alongside a pretty nutcracker

Corn nuts

Olives | and if you do end up wanting to follow a very simple recipe to make them spicy, head to page 47

Moitié-Moitié | a little plate of very good anchovies + chunks of Parmesan cheese

Sun-dried tomatoes | drizzle with a little of your top-shelf olive oil and a pinch of freshly ground black or pink peppercorns

Charcuterie | + cornichons + grainy mustard

Chili mango

Cheese twists, crackers, taralli

Store-bought spreads, such as tapenade, hummus, or tarama (taramosalata)

Good bread with butter served as if it's cheese | a.k.a. The Peppler

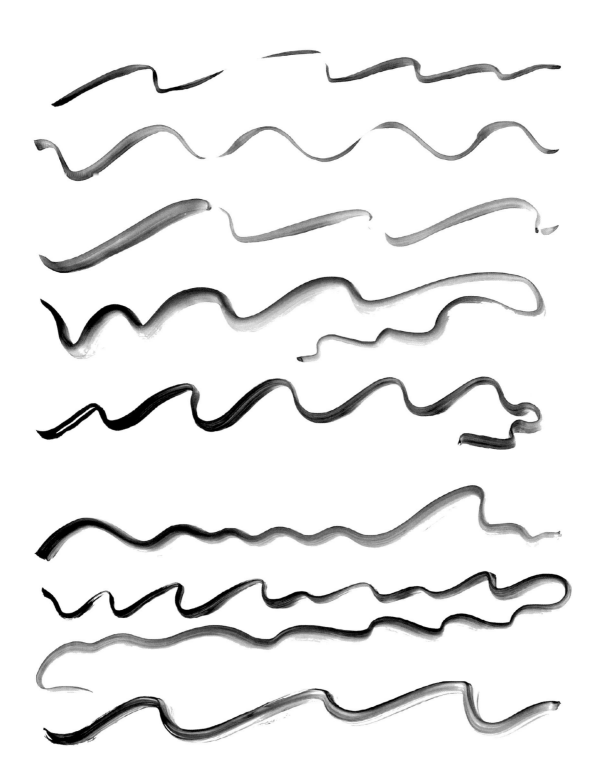

to CONTINUE

TO CONTINUE

MEAT + SEAFOOD

Market Day Roast Chicken + Potatoes

Find me at any and all markets in Provence, woven baskets and cotton totes a-swinging. But it's really about the markets that feel like they overtake a whole town. Wednesdays in Saint-Rémy-de-Provence is one such. The people and stalls wind through the streets, snaking down alleyways, a party of olives and greens and flowers and melons and cheeses backing up against shops and cafés and shady squares. And there is always a true soul-favorite: potatoes cooked under roasting, spinning, browning, dripping poulet rôti. You can buy them separate from their chicken collaborators and enjoy the flavor of roast chicken once removed, something I do often to add to a grand aïoli (page 181). Or you can buy both poulet and poulet-y potatoes and serve them together. This roast chicken is my closest approximation to those potatoes, here spatchcocked and laid flat over the potatoes to grasp as many surface-level drippings as possible.

Serves 6

Preheat the oven to 425°F [220°C].

Pat the chicken dry with paper towels. Season all over with salt and pepper and set aside for at least 30 minutes at room temperature (you can also season the chicken the night before and remove from the refrigerator about 1 hour before cooking).

On a rimmed baking sheet or in a large ceramic baking dish, toss together the potatoes and shallots with 2 tablespoons of the olive oil and season with salt and pepper. Add the garlic and lemon halves to the center of the dish and drizzle with the wine. Place the tarragon sprigs on top. Place the chicken, breast-side up, on top in the center of the dish and drizzle with the remaining 2 tablespoons of olive oil. Roast until the chicken is cooked through and the potatoes are browned and very tender, 40 to 50 minutes. Remove from the oven and let the chicken rest for 10 minutes before serving. Just before serving, squeeze the garlic cloves from the halves and toss with the potatoes. Squeeze the lemon halves over the potatoes and discard. Serve warm. CONTINUED

One 3- to 4-pound [1.4 to 1.8 kg] chicken, spatchcocked (see Note)

Fine sea salt

Freshly ground black pepper

1½ pounds [680 g] very small waxy potatoes

10 shallots, halved (large shallots quartered)

4 tablespoons [60 ml] extra-virgin olive oil

2 garlic heads, unpeeled and halved crosswise

2 medium lemons, halved crosswise

⅓ cup [80 ml] dry white wine

4 sprigs fresh tarragon (see Note)

note to spatchcock the chicken | To spatchcock a chicken, use a pair of very sharp kitchen shears (or a sharp knife) to cut along both sides of the backbone. Remove the backbone—save it for stock! (see Note below)—and open up the bird so it lies flat.

note | If you don't have ready access to it, you can use another herb for the tarragon. Rosemary or thyme sprigs are particularly lovely.

note to make the chicken stock | While I prepare chicken stock differently every time based on whatever else I have in the house, the basic route from one night's roast chicken to a freezer full of stock is straightforward: Take **the chicken bones** and **the backbone** you saved while spatchcocking, add them to a pot to slow simmer with **some water** and **any vegetable trimmings** (onion peels, shallot peels, carrot peels, that stick of celery that's getting limp in the back of the produce drawer, fennel tops, parsley stems), **a few crushed garlic cloves, a tablespoon or two of whole black peppercorns, another of whole coriander seeds** (unless you have fresh cilantro stems, then use those), **a bay leaf or two**, and maybe **a whole clove or star anise or dried chili** for another layer of flavor. Really, it's up to you. Just leave it unsalted until it's in whatever recipe you decide to put it in.

Pastis Chicken

One very chilly fall day, a dear friend invited me to dinner at her beautiful home in Lacoste (a village in the Luberon crowned by an eleventh-century château that was home to the Marquis de Sade in the late 1700s and later owned by the couturier Pierre Cardin). Somewhere between invite and arrival, the weeknight dinner turned dinner party, with a long table bedecked with local flowers and the platonic ideal of vintage linens and serving ware running the length of her living room straight into the kitchen. Ruth made gin and tonics, pavlova, and a chicken that was not this chicken. But I wrote this chicken recipe for and by channeling her.

Serves 6 to 8

4 pounds [1.8 kg] chicken thighs (about eight 8-ounce [230 g] thighs)

Fine sea salt

2 tablespoons extra-virgin olive oil

2 medium shallots, thinly sliced

2 medium fennel bulbs, trimmed and thinly sliced, fronds reserved

Freshly ground black pepper

4 garlic cloves, finely chopped

2 sprigs fresh thyme

1 lemon, halved crosswise

¼ cup [60 ml] pastis (see Note)

2 tablespoons unsalted European butter, cut into small pieces

Preheat the oven to 400°F [200°C].

Pat the chicken thighs dry with a paper towel and season with salt (you can also season the chicken the night before and remove from the refrigerator about 1 hour before cooking). In a Dutch oven or large ovenproof skillet over medium heat, add the oil. When the oil is hot, add the chicken pieces in a single layer to the pot, working in batches, and cook until well browned on both sides, 6 to 8 minutes on each side. Transfer to a plate and repeat until all the chicken is browned.

Add the shallots to the pot and cook, stirring occasionally, until tender and translucent, 3 to 5 minutes. Add the fennel, season with salt and pepper, and cook until the fennel starts to soften, 6 to 8 minutes more. Stir in the garlic and thyme sprigs; season with salt. Cook for 2 minutes, then remove the pot from the heat. Nestle the lemon halves, cut-side down, into the fennel mixture until they press onto the bottom of the pot. Pour the pastis into the pot and add the chicken as well as any juices that have collected on the plate, nestling it into the fennel mixture. Dot with the butter. Roast in the oven until the chicken is cooked through and a deep golden brown, 20 to 25 minutes. CONTINUED

Transfer the chicken to a plate and set aside to rest for a few minutes. If the fennel mixture is still a little too liquidy, continue to cook on the stovetop over medium-high heat until the liquid evaporates a bit more, then spoon the fennel mixture onto a serving platter and squeeze the juice from one of the lemon halves over the top. Season with salt and pepper. Arrange the chicken on top of the fennel and squeeze the juice of the other lemon half over the chicken. Serve warm.

note | If you're not a pastis lover, fear not this recipe. The liqueur boosts the sweet, herbal notes of the fennel and shallots without leaving you feeling like you're sitting down to drink a tall glass of anise. If you are a pastis lover, you'll likely have some left in your bottle after making this recipe— might I suggest a round of Marseillans (page 28)?

Poulet à l'Ail

GARLIC CHICKEN

The first chicken I cooked in Julia Child's Provençal kitchen was this chicken, thus creating a core taste memory that will forever speak to my PBS-gripped childhood heart. I regret to say I did not make my poulet dance in that iconic pegboarded kitchen, but I did pour myself the last of the wine and lingered before bed at the tall center countertop stacking together bits of tender meat and wilted parsley on top of thick slices of bread, toasted in drippings and spread with roasted garlic. I made a bit more mess in the process, which I think JC would have appreciated.

One 3- to 4-pound [1.4 to 1.8 kg] chicken

Fine sea salt

Freshly ground black pepper

1 yellow onion, quartered

3 sprigs fresh rosemary

2 bay leaves

2 garlic heads, unpeeled and halved crosswise

6 tablespoons [90 ml] extra-virgin olive oil

2 tablespoons unsalted European butter, at room temperature

8 one-inch [2.5 cm] thick slices crusty bread

1 tablespoon Dijon mustard

2 large bunches fresh flat-leaf parsley, leaves picked

2 tablespoons sherry or red wine vinegar

Serves 6

Preheat the oven to 325°F [165°C].

Pat the chicken dry with paper towels. Season all over with salt and pepper and set aside for at least 30 minutes at room temperature (you can also season the chicken the night before and remove from the refrigerator about 1 hour before cooking). Place the onion quarters, one rosemary sprig, and the bay leaves in the cavity of the chicken. Tie the legs together with kitchen twine.

In a large cast-iron skillet or small roasting pan, add the garlic halves and remaining 2 rosemary sprigs and drizzle with 2 tablespoons of the olive oil. Place the chicken, breast-side up, on top. Rub the butter all over the chicken, then drizzle with 2 tablespoons of olive oil. Roast until the chicken is deep golden brown and cooked through and the juices run clear, 1½ to 2 hours. Transfer the chicken and garlic halves to a cutting board, leaving the juices in the pan, and set aside to rest for 15 minutes. CONTINUED

Place a large skillet or grill pan over medium-high heat. Use a pastry brush to brush both sides of the bread slices with the pan drippings, then place in the skillet and toast until golden and crisp on both sides. While the bread toasts, pour any remaining pan drippings into a small bowl. Squeeze the roasted garlic from the garlic halves into the bowl, add the mustard, and smash together to combine. Spread on the toasted bread.

Scatter the parsley leaves on a serving platter. Drizzle with vinegar and the remaining 2 tablespoons of olive oil. Season with salt and pepper. Place the warm chicken on top of the parsley and serve with the toasted, garlicked bread.

Moules in Aïoli

I'm certain there are plenty of small, cute beach shacks on France's southeastern coast where you can get mussels and fries and drink rosé and pastis with your friends or your lover or alone. But *my* favorite small, cute beach shack is tucked directly into the seawall (?!) about 20 minutes south of Marseille's city center, and *they* toss their mussels in aïoli. Do that here, and add fries (page 195).

Serves 6

In a large pot or Dutch oven over medium heat, add the oil. Once the oil is hot, add the shallots and garlic and cook, stirring, until the shallots are translucent, about 5 minutes. Season with salt and pepper and pour in the wine. Let simmer, uncovered, for 5 minutes.

Add the mussels to the pot and use a wooden spoon to stir them into the shallot mixture. Cover the pot and cook, stirring halfway through, until the mussels are opened and fully cooked, 6 to 8 minutes.

Transfer the mussels to a serving bowl, reserving the broth. Strain the broth through a fine-mesh sieve, discarding the solids. Add the aïoli to a small bowl and gradually whisk in 3 tablespoons of the mussel broth. Spoon the sauce over the mussels, tossing to coat, and serve with crusty bread.

3 tablespoons extra-virgin olive oil

4 shallots, thinly sliced

2 garlic cloves, thinly sliced

Fine sea salt

Freshly ground black pepper

¼ cup [60 ml] dry white wine or vermouth

4 pounds [1.8 kg] mussels (see Note)

1 cup [240 ml] aïoli, (page 181), for serving

Crusty bread, for serving

note to prepare the mussels | Place them in a colander or fine-mesh sieve and rinse with cold water. Scrub gently to remove any grit and use your hands to remove the "beard" (the thread-like piece attached to the side of the shells) by tugging firmly. If any mussels are open and don't close when tapped, discard them. Drain and transfer to a large bowl.

note | Should you like, this dish can be, and often is, also served chilled.

Clams + Raïto

Traditionally you'll find fish (salt cod, halibut, haddock, eel) simmering in raïto, but one day in line at the fishmonger in Saint-Saturnin-lès-Apt—a small, storybook village in the Luberon Valley—I found myself staring down a glistening jumble of ridged clams. Tomatoes, onions, garlic, and thyme already in my basket; raïto already in mind; I pictured the shells spread open, releasing their straight-from-the-sea liquor in exchange for a clutch of the caper and olive-studded sauce. I continued thwarting tradition by using sweet vermouth in place of raïto's classic red wine—the swap further intensifies the dish's herbal undertones. (Worth noting here as much as anywhere: I know how ridiculous my stories sound sometimes! But they're all real!)

¼ cup [60 ml] extra-virgin olive oil

2 yellow onions, finely chopped

Fine sea salt

2 tablespoons all-purpose flour

3 cups [720 ml] sweet vermouth or dry red wine

6 plum tomatoes, chopped

5 garlic cloves, peeled and crushed

4 sprigs fresh thyme

2 bay leaves

Freshly ground black pepper

3 pounds [1.4 kg] small clams, such as littlenecks, scrubbed clean (see Note)

½ cup [80 g] Niçoise olives, Nyon olives, or other cured black olives

2 tablespoons salted capers, rinsed, drained, and finely chopped

½ cup [20 g] finely chopped fresh flat-leaf parsley

Crusty bread, for serving

Serves 6 to 8

In a medium pot or Dutch oven set over medium heat, heat the oil until hot. Add the onions and season with salt. Cook, stirring often, until the onions are soft and lightly golden, about 20 minutes. Add the flour and cook, stirring, for 3 minutes, then pour in a few tablespoons of the vermouth, stirring to combine. Continue slowly adding the vermouth, stirring constantly. Once all the vermouth is added, add 1 cup [240 ml] of water, the tomatoes, garlic, thyme, and bay leaves. Season with pepper. Bring to a strong simmer and cook, stirring occasionally, until the sauce is thickened and reduced by half, 1 to 1½ hours.

Stir in the clams, olives, and capers. Bring to a boil, then cover the pot with a tight-fitting lid, lower the heat to medium-low, and simmer until the clams open, 10 to 12 minutes. Uncover, remove and discard any clams that don't open, and add half of the parsley. Stir to combine and taste for seasoning, then transfer to a serving platter. Sprinkle with the remaining parsley. Serve with crusty bread.

note | If you can't find littlenecks, use Manila clams or even cockles (a small, sweet, clam-like bivalve). If you're lucky to find tellines—small and colorful and called "wedge clams" in English—they're especially delicious in this one.

Paella Camarguaise

5 cups [1.2 L] chicken stock, store-bought or homemade (see Note, page 96)

½ cup [120 ml] dry white wine

½ teaspoon saffron threads, gently crushed with your fingertips or with a mortar and pestle

¼ cup [60 ml] extra-virgin olive oil

1 large yellow onion, diced

Fine sea salt

2 garlic cloves, finely chopped

2 roasted red peppers, thinly sliced (store-bought or see page 167)

3 large tomatoes, coarsely chopped

2 cups [400 g] long-grain white rice, preferably from the Camargue

8 ounces [230 g] large shrimp (16 to 20), deveined

8 ounces [230 g] mussels (to prepare, see Note, page 107)

8 ounces [230 g] small clams, such as littlenecks, scrubbed clean

2 tablespoons unsalted European butter, cut into cubes

3 tablespoons finely chopped fresh flat-leaf parsley

Lemon wedges, for serving

When I was working on the edits for my first book, *Apéritif*, a friend of mine spent a few months cooking in Arles. Not one to throw away a chance to hop on a train for food or sunshine, I packed the manuscript and spent a few days unrolling it at a café in the main square around the corner from her apartment. Hunger is one of my top procrastination crutches, and so I also spent plenty of time wandering the stone streets and alleys of the ancient city, stumbling onto Roman ruins, vantage points favored by van Gogh, and massive pans of paella. Rice, cultivated in the Camargue wetlands just south of Arles since the sixteenth century, lies at its base, the plump, creamy grains made yellow and fragrant by saffron and studded with mussels, clams, and bright red shrimp. Shopping, prepping, and cooking this recipe is also great if you have something to put off.

Serves 8

In a large pot over medium heat, combine the chicken stock, the wine, and saffron. Bring to a simmer, then turn off the heat, cover, and keep warm.

In a 12-inch [30.5 cm] skillet or paella pan over medium-high heat, heat the oil until hot. Add the onion and season with salt. Cook, stirring often, until the onion is translucent, about 10 minutes. Add the garlic and continue to cook for 1 minute more. Stir in the peppers and tomatoes and cook for 3 minutes, then stir in the rice, making sure the grains are well coated in the mixture. Slowly pour in the warm stock, wine, and saffron, reserving 1 cup [240 ml], and season lightly with salt. Bring to a simmer, then cook, without stirring, for 15 minutes. CONTINUED

Season the shrimp with salt, then arrange the shrimp, mussels, and clams on top of the rice. Scatter the butter cubes on top and pour the remaining 1 cup [240 ml] of the stock mixture over the top, then cover the skillet tightly with a lid or foil. Cook until the mussels and clams open, 15 to 20 minutes. Remove the skillet from the heat, discard any mussels and clams that didn't open, sprinkle with the parsley, and serve with lemon wedges.

note | Shocking to no one, Camargue rice is the star in paella Camarguaise. Unlike its Spanish counterpart, paella in the Camargue uses long-grain Camargue rice rather than short grain. If you can't find true Camargue rice (look online!) use another long-grain white rice in this recipe.

La Bourride

FOR THE FISH STOCK

1 to 1½ pounds [455 to 680 g] fish bones and/or fish heads from fish fillets

1 leek, sliced

1 onion, chopped

1 small fennel bulb, chopped

4 garlic cloves, smashed

¾ cup [180 ml] dry white wine

1 tablespoon whole black peppercorns

½ teaspoon fennel seed

1 bay leaf

One 3-inch [7.5 cm] orange peel

FOR THE AÏOLI

4 large egg yolks

1 to 2 small garlic cloves, grated on a Microplane

¼ cup [60 ml] grapeseed or canola oil

½ cup [120 ml] extra-virgin olive oil

Fine sea salt

FOR THE CROUTONS

1 baguette, thinly sliced

Extra-virgin olive oil

1 garlic clove, halved crosswise

FOR LA BOURRIDE

2½ pounds [1.2 kg] firm white-fleshed fish fillets, such as halibut, sea bass, monkfish, cod, or sea bream or a mix

Fine sea salt

1½ pounds [680 g] mussels (to prepare, see Note, page 107)

Bouillabaisse takes up a lot of space in the conversation of Provençal fish stews, and that's fine, but allow me to introduce bourride. She comes with fewer rules and more unctuous body than her better-known cousin, and to know her is to love her. The heady, herbal fish broth is enriched with enough thick aïoli to turn the base voluptuous and is served with flaky white fish and mussels. If you like, make extra aïoli to serve on the side. She's so hot, this one.

Serves 6

To make the fish stock: In a large Dutch oven or pot over medium heat, add the fish bones and heads, leek, onion, fennel, garlic cloves, wine, peppercorns, fennel seed, bay leaf, and orange peel. Pour in 5 cups [1.2 L] of water. Bring to a boil, then lower the heat and simmer for about 1 hour, skimming off any scum that rises to the surface every now and then. Strain the stock through a fine-mesh sieve, pressing on and discarding the solids. The stock can be made and stored in the refrigerator up to 24 hours in advance.

To make the aïoli: In a medium bowl, whisk together the yolks and garlic. Whisking constantly, add the grapeseed oil drop by drop until the mixture thickens. Continuing to whisk constantly, pour in the olive oil in a slow, steady stream. The aïoli should be very thick. Season with salt. The aïoli can be made and stored in the refrigerator up to 24 hours in advance.

To make the croutons: Preheat the oven to 350°F [180°C]. Arrange the baguette slices on a baking sheet and drizzle or brush the tops with olive oil. Bake until the slices are crisp and lightly golden (this is more to dry them out than to toast them), 8 to 10 minutes. Remove from the oven and rub with the cut sides of the garlic.

To make la bourride: Season the fish fillets with salt. Pour the strained fish stock into a Dutch oven or heavy pot, bring to a simmer, and lightly season with fine sea salt. Gently add the fillets and mussels to the pot, cover, and cook until the mussels are opened and fully cooked and the fish fillets are just cooked through, 6 to 8 minutes. Uncover and gently remove the seafood with a slotted spoon, discarding any mussels that didn't open, and transfer to a serving platter or bowl.

Whisking constantly, slowly add about ¼ cup [60 ml] of the hot broth to the aïoli. Once fully combined, slowly add another ¼ cup [60 ml], whisking constantly. Add a final ¼ cup [60 ml], then slowly add the thinned aïoli to the pot. Cook over medium-low heat, stirring constantly, for 10 to 15 minutes. Remove from the heat. Divide the croutons, fish, and mussels among warm bowls and ladle the bourride over the top. Serve immediately with extra croutons.

note | You can use one kind of fish or a wide variety in la bourride. Ask your fishmonger to choose whatever is freshest, then debone and fillet the chosen tribute for you, reserving the bones and maybe tossing in a few extras to flavor your stock.

Whole Roasted Fish

A whole roasted fish, all to yourself, may conjure holidays by the sea. Just me? Well, I have many such memories on the Côte d'Azur, toes in sand, rosé all around, house music doing what it does, out-of-office on. But the choicest whole roasted fish I've eaten in this lifetime was bought in the river-woven town of L'Isle-sur-la-Sorgue and cooked at a friend's inland home on a weeknight. For the most ease, ask your fishmonger to clean and scale whatever is freshest and make this version, prettily stuffed with lemon slices and a simple pistou.

Serves 6

Preheat the oven to 475°F [240°C].

In a large skillet over medium heat, add 3 tablespoons of the oil. Once the oil is hot, add the shallots and cook, stirring, until tender and golden, about 5 minutes. Add the red pepper flakes and cook for 30 seconds more. Remove the skillet from the heat and set aside to cool slightly. Stir in the pistou and the lemon zest from one of the lemons. Season with fine sea salt and pepper.

Pat the fish dry and season with fine sea salt and pepper, inside and out. Thinly slice one of the lemons; remove and discard the seeds. Stuff each fish cavity with 3 or 4 lemon slices, then tuck 1 to 1½ tablespoons of the shallot-pistou mixture into each cavity and arrange the fish in a single layer on a baking sheet. Drizzle each fish with a tablespoon of the remaining olive oil and place in the oven. Roast until the flesh is opaque and flaky, 15 to 20 minutes. Transfer to a serving platter, drizzle with olive oil, and sprinkle with flaky sea salt. Cut the remaining lemon into wedges and serve with the fish. CONTINUED

9 tablespoons [135 ml] extra-virgin olive oil, plus more for serving

4 shallots, thinly sliced

Pinch red pepper flakes

½ cup [120 ml] A Very Classic Pistou (recipe follows)

2 lemons

Fine sea salt

Freshly ground black pepper

Six 1 pound [455 g] whole sea bass, branzino, or rainbow trout, cleaned and scaled

Flaky sea salt

A Very Classic Pistou

Makes ½ cup [120 ml]

If you are making the pistou with a mortar and pestle:
Place the garlic and salt in a mortar and grind until a paste
forms. Add the basil leaves by the handful and pound them,
scraping the sides of the mortar often, until they are almost
smooth and all the basil is incorporated. Slowly add the oil,
1 tablespoon at a time, smashing until it's all combined.
Season with salt to taste.

    If you are making the pistou with a blender: Place
the garlic cloves in the blender and pulse until roughly
chopped. Add the salt and basil and pulse, scraping the
sides of the blender often, until nearly smooth. With
the blender running, slowly pour in the oil until it's all
combined. Season with salt.

    The pistou can be made and stored in an airtight
container in the refrigerator for up to 3 days in advance.

2 garlic cloves

½ teaspoon flaky sea salt,
plus more to taste

3 cups [75 g] basil leaves

⅓ cup [80 ml] extra-virgin
olive oil

Poisson Froid Mayonnaise

I am not one for the club. As you know already, though, I am one for the beach. Which is one of the reasons I found myself a few summers back surrounded by tamarisk trees and oversized baskets of crudités and Dior bags sitting down to lunch at Le Club 55 in Saint-Tropez. The historic beach club and restaurant has arguably been the longest-running scene on Pampelonne Beach since Brigitte Bardot's day in the Saint-Tropez sun, the sky-blue tables and sun loungers packed (and still packed) with the kind of people you know but you don't *know* know. Much more important to this writer's story, it's the scene where I first ate what I've come to think of as the simplest, finest summer lunch: a poached fillet of fish, served chilled with mayonnaise, a side of hot fries (page 195), and cold rosé.

FOR THE COURT BOUILLON

4 garlic cloves

2 medium carrots, peeled and chopped

1 yellow onion, coarsely chopped

8 to 10 sprigs fresh parsley

6 sprigs fresh thyme

1 bay leaf

Fine sea salt

2 cups [480 ml] dry white wine

10 whole black peppercorns

10 whole coriander seeds

FOR THE FISH

Six 6- to 8-ounce [170 to 230 g] mild, boneless, skinless fish fillets, such as cod, halibut, sea bass, or hake

Fine sea salt

Mayonnaise (recipe follows)

Serves 6

To make the court bouillon: In a large pot over high heat, combine 8 cups [2 L] of water, the garlic, carrots, onion, parsley, thyme, and bay leaf. Season lightly with salt. Bring to a boil, then lower the heat and simmer for 15 minutes. Add the wine, peppercorns, and coriander seeds and continue to simmer for another 15 minutes. Strain the liquid through a fine-mesh sieve, pressing lightly on the vegetables to extract the flavors; discard the solids. Set aside to cool to room temperature, then use or refrigerate, covered, for 2 days (or freeze for up to 1 month).

To make the fish: Season the fish fillets with salt. Gently place the pieces in the bottom of a large, high-sided skillet. Pour in the cooled court bouillon and place over medium-low heat. Bring to just a simmer, then cover the pan, lower the heat to low, and cook until the fish is opaque and just cooked through (a thin knife inserted into the center of the pieces should be met with little resistance), 4 to 6 minutes. Use a slotted spoon or spatula to gently remove the fillets and transfer to a plate, cover loosely, and refrigerate until chilled completely (for at least 2 hours and up to 8 hours) before serving. Serve with mayonnaise.

CONTINUED

Mayonnaise

Makes about 1 cup [240 ml]

In a medium bowl, whisk together the yolks and mustard. Whisking constantly, add the grapeseed oil drop by drop until the mixture thickens. Continuing to whisk constantly, pour in the remaining grapeseed oil and the olive oil in a slow, steady stream. Add the lemon juice in teaspoon increments, whisking constantly. The mayonnaise should be pale yellow and thick. Season with salt and more lemon juice as needed. Transfer to a serving bowl.

note | Add finely chopped capers, preserved lemon, anchovies, herbs, piment d'Espelette, or whatever else you like to your mayonnaise as desired.

2 large egg yolks

1½ teaspoons Dijon mustard

¼ cup [60 ml] grapeseed or canola oil

½ cup [120 ml] extra-virgin olive oil

1 to 2 tablespoons fresh lemon juice, plus more as needed

Fine sea salt

Daube Provençal

Dora Maar, the experimental, radical surrealist artist and photographer, bought a house in Ménerbes in 1944. The medieval, walled hilltop village with sweeping views of vineyards and olive trees is where she chose to spend her summers following a breakup (with Picasso). Ménerbes remains a really good place to go through a breakup. My first memory of Maar's home—now an artist residency—was in moody mid-winter, and I ate daube provençal.

3½ pounds [1.6 kg] boneless beef shoulder, shank, chuck, or a mixture, cut into 1½- to 2-inch [4 to 5 cm] pieces

Fine sea salt

Freshly ground black pepper

4 ounces [115 g] pancetta or unsmoked bacon, cut into ½-inch [12 mm] pieces

6 garlic cloves, peeled and crushed

2 tablespoons extra-virgin olive oil

2 medium yellow onions, thinly sliced

1 medium carrot, sliced diagonally into 1-inch [2.5 cm] thick slices

1 celery stalk, sliced diagonally into 1-inch [2.5 cm] thick slices

10 sprigs fresh parsley

6 sprigs fresh thyme

2 bay leaves

Two 3-inch [7.5 cm] strips orange peel, fresh or dried (see Note)

One 750 ml bottle dry red wine

4 medium plum tomatoes (or one 14-ounce [400 g] can crushed tomatoes)

¼ cup [60 ml] cognac or brandy

Cooked white beans, pasta, or crusty bread, for serving

Serves 6 to 8

In a large bowl, add the cubes of beef and season with salt and pepper. Add the pancetta and 3 of the garlic cloves along with the olive oil, half of the onion slices, the carrot, celery, 5 of the parsley sprigs, 4 of the thyme sprigs, 1 of the bay leaves, and 1 of the orange peels. Pour the wine over the top, cover, and set aside to marinate for 2 hours at room temperature (or overnight in the refrigerator).

Strain the marinade into another bowl, discarding the marinade's garlic, onions, carrots, celery, herbs, and orange peel. Cut a piece of parchment paper into a circle that just fits inside a large Dutch oven or pot with a tight-fitting lid.

In the large Dutch oven or pot, add half of the beef mixture in an even layer. With kitchen twine or in a cheesecloth, tie together the remaining 5 parsley sprigs, 2 thyme sprigs, 1 bay leaf, and 1 orange peel. Finely chop the remaining 3 garlic cloves and add to the pot along with the herb sachet/bouquet garni, the remaining sliced onion, and the tomatoes in an even layer on top of the beef. Season with salt. Add the remaining beef mixture on top and pour the cognac and reserved marinade over the top. If needed, add a little water to just cover the meat. Slowly bring to a boil over medium heat. Skim off any foam that rises to the surface, then reduce the heat to a very bare simmer. Set the parchment paper circle on top, pressing gently to remove any air bubbles, and cover the pot. Cook, regulating the heat as needed so the liquid stays at a very gentle simmer (boiling toughens the meat), until the meat is extremely tender and the sauce is rich, 4 to 5 hours. CONTINUED

If serving immediately, skim as much fat off the top as possible before serving. If serving the next day (which is preferred! See Note!), let the daube cool to room temperature, then cover and refrigerate overnight. The next day, skim any hardened fat from the top and gently reheat before serving. Serve with cooked white beans, pasta, or crusty bread.

notes on daube

- Like all of us, daube gets better with dedicated time for rest. Make it the day before you want to eat it. The next day, when the flavors of the daube have deepened, all you need to do is rewarm and indulge fully in the delayed gratification that is yesterday's forethought.

- Some add cured black olives to their daube provençal. If this appeals, pit the olives and add to the pot about 30 minutes before you are ready to serve, allowing them to warm through.

- The orange peels in this dish are a specifically Provençal addition. Traditionally the peel is from a bitter Seville orange, though a navel orange works just as well if that's all you have access to. Should you come across a pile of Seville oranges, do yourself a favor and buy a crate. Peel a few with a vegetable peeler (leaving the white pith behind) and set the peels out to dry thoroughly, about 3 days, then store in an airtight container in a cool, dark place for future daubes (the dried peels will keep up to 2 years). Use the rest of your crate to make Vin d'Orange (page 36).

- Daube is traditionally made in a daubière, a wide-at-the-base, narrow-at-the-neck earthenware pot. Sans daubière, using a large, heavy pot or Dutch oven with a tight-fitting lid and cutting a circle of parchment paper to set directly on top of the daube will mimic the effect of a daubière, reducing evaporation and concentrating flavors.

LA MACARONADE

Should you find yourself with leftover sauce at the end of the meal, save it and transform it into the parsimonious luxury that is la macaronade:

Cook **1 pound [455 g] of short macaroni or another small, short pasta** in boiling, salted water until al dente. Transfer to a large buttered baking dish and add **1½ to 2 cups [360 to 480 ml] of the reserved sauce from the daube (and any bits of leftover meat), 2 tablespoons of unsalted European butter, a pinch of freshly grated nutmeg,** and **½ cup [15 g] of freshly grated Parmigiano-Reggiano**. Mix to combine, then top with another **½ cup [15 g] of freshly grated Parmigiano-Reggiano**. You can cover and refrigerate this for up to 2 days before placing it under the broiler until the top is lightly browned and crisp. Eat warm.

La Broufade

While Provence may be more often portrayed as a sunny, hot, perpetual summer holiday, winter is very real here, chilled even further by le mistral. The intense, sometimes bitterly cold wind pulls air from the foothills of the Alps and rushes down river valleys to the sea, bending trees in its wake, churning waters, and driving everyone inside for daube. While you'll most often find daube made with red wine (page 127), la broufade, also called broufaddo or l'aigriade saint-gilloise or fricot des barques, enlists the rarer white. The pungent combination of cornichons, capers, and anchovies is the key to the deeply complex, immensely satisfying dish with long-simmering ancestral roots in the Camargue (it was traditionally prepared in advance and eaten by mariners working for days at a time on the Rhône River).

3½ pounds [1.6 kg] boneless beef chuck, trimmed and cut into 1-inch [2.5 cm] pieces

6 tablespoons [90 ml] extra-virgin olive oil

8 garlic cloves, finely chopped

2 bay leaves

Pinch freshly grated nutmeg

Fine sea salt

Freshly ground black pepper

8 sprigs fresh thyme

2 whole cloves

3 medium yellow onions, thinly sliced

One 14-ounce [400 g] can whole, peeled tomatoes, crushed

15 cornichons, chopped

2 tablespoons salted capers, soaked, rinsed, drained, and coarsely chopped

6 anchovies packed in olive oil, coarsely chopped

One 750 ml bottle dry white wine

Cooked long-grain white rice, preferably from the Camargue, for serving

Serves 6 to 8

In a large bowl, add the beef, olive oil, garlic, bay leaves, and nutmeg. Season very lightly with salt and pepper, stirring to combine. Cover the bowl, and set aside to marinate for 2 hours at room temperature (or overnight in the refrigerator).

Preheat the oven to 325°F [165°C]. Cut a piece of parchment paper into a circle that just fits inside a large Dutch oven or pot with a tight-fitting lid. Remove the bay leaves from the marinade and wrap them in cheesecloth with the thyme and cloves. Reserve.

In a separate large bowl, combine the onions, tomatoes, cornichons, capers, and anchovies. Add about a third of the onion-tomato mixture to the bottom of the Dutch oven or pot and season lightly with pepper. Top with about a third of the beef. Repeat this layering twice more, ending with the beef. Add the prepared herb sachet and any remaining juices from the marinade to the pot, then pour in the wine; the liquid should just cover the mixture. CONTINUED

Place over medium-high heat and bring to a simmer, then place the parchment paper circle on top, pressing gently to remove any air bubbles, and cover the pot. Transfer to the oven and cook, regulating the heat as needed so the liquid stays at a very gentle simmer (boiling toughens the meat) until the meat is extremely tender and the sauce is rich and thick, about 4 hours. Remove from the oven, discard the herb sachet, and season with salt and pepper. Serve immediately or let cool to room temperature and refrigerate overnight. The next day, skim any hardened fat from the top, and gently reheat before serving. Serve with rice. La broufade will keep covered, in the refrigerator, for a few days.

Steak à la Beurre d'Anchois

This one is for a night when you want to, like, *do a thing*, but you don't want to *leave the house*. Instead, splurge at the good butcher shop, put on something that makes you feel extra, gather the good people, light some candles, and start with a round of Martinis Provençal (page 32). The key to tender, perfectly cooked, beautifully crusty steaks is to hover, turning the steaks frequently, basting them in the herby anchovy butter. Please don't fear the anchovies; they dissolve into the buttery, herby, garlicky juices as the steaks cook, creating an umami-rich sauce, a secret surf and turf, as it were.

Serves 6

Pat the steaks dry with paper towels and season generously with salt. Set aside at room temperature for at least 45 minutes or refrigerate, loosely covered, overnight. When you're ready to cook, remove the steaks from the refrigerator and let sit at room temperature for 30 to 45 minutes.

In a small bowl, use a fork to mash together the butter and anchovies.

Set a large cast-iron skillet over high heat and add 2 tablespoons of the vegetable oil. Once the pan is hot and the oil is starting to smoke, carefully add one of the steaks and cook, flipping the steak frequently (every 30 seconds to a minute or so), for 4 to 5 minutes, until a lightly golden crust starts to form. Add half of the anchovy butter, 2 garlic cloves, half of the shallots, and 1 sprig of rosemary to the skillet and lower the heat to medium. Continue to cook, flipping the steaks occasionally, using a spoon to baste the steak with the butter. Continue until the steaks are medium-rare (a thermometer inserted into the thickest part should register 120°F to 125°F [50°C to 52°C]), 6 to 8 minutes more.

Transfer to a large heatproof plate or platter and pour the pan juices over the top. Wipe out the skillet and repeat with the remaining steak, anchovy butter, garlic, shallots, and rosemary. Cut the steaks away from the bone and slice against the grain into ½- to ¾-inch [12 mm to 2 cm] slices. Serve warm.

Two 1½- to 2-pound [680 to 910 g] bone-in rib-eye or strip loin steaks, about 1½ inches [4 cm] thick

Kosher salt

6 tablespoons [85 g] unsalted European butter

12 anchovies, finely chopped

4 tablespoons [60 ml] vegetable oil

4 garlic cloves, smashed and peeled

2 medium shallots, thinly sliced

2 sprigs rosemary

Lamb for Joann

Lamb for Joann is, you guessed it, for Joann. Long before the exact form of this book took shape, I promised the always hungry, eternally brilliant, tabletop-climbing, dirty joke— and lamb-loving photographer of this book (and the one before that and the one before that) a really good lamb recipe. Luckily, when the scope of *le SUD* came into focus, a rich, soft, supple, earthy, herbal leg of lamb wasn't hard to place. L'agneau always belongs at the southern French table, and Sisteron lamb in particular—that is PGI (Protected Geographical Indication) designated and grazes on the lush wild grasses and herbs of Haute Provence—is especially and rightfully famed. Joann, this gigot d'agneau, made with aromatics of the region and not a small amount of vermouth, is for you, with love.

Serves 6

One 4- to 5-pound [1.8 to 2.3 kg] bone-in leg of lamb, trimmed and patted dry with paper towels

5 garlic cloves, peeled and thinly sliced

Fine sea salt

Freshly ground black pepper

¼ cup [60 ml] extra-virgin olive oil

2 pounds [910 g] new potatoes, cleaned and halved

8 ounces [230 g] shallots (8 to 10), peeled and halved

2 tablespoons grainy mustard

2 cups [480 ml] dry vermouth, dry white wine, or fino sherry

8 sprigs fresh thyme

4 sprigs fresh rosemary

4 sprigs fresh tarragon, if desired

2 bay leaves

Preheat the oven to 300°F [150°C].

Use a sharp paring knife to cut slits all over the lamb, each about 1½ inches [4 cm] deep. Use your finger to press a slice of garlic into each incision (you should use about 2 of the garlic cloves). Season the lamb generously with salt and pepper.

Add the oil to a large Dutch oven or heavy ovenproof pot with a tight-fitting lid over medium-high heat. Once the oil is hot, add the lamb and sear until browned on all sides, about 10 minutes. Remove the pot from the heat and transfer the lamb to a large plate; set aside.

Add the potatoes to the pot, as many cut-sides down as possible, and season with salt and pepper. Cook, without stirring, until the potatoes are golden on the cut sides, about 10 minutes. Add the shallots and stir together, cooking for 5 minutes more. Stir in the remaining garlic, the mustard, vermouth, thyme sprigs, rosemary sprigs, tarragon (if using), and bay leaves, using a wooden spoon to scrape up any brown bits from the bottom of the pan.

CONTINUED

Return the lamb leg to the Dutch oven, cover, and transfer to the oven. Cook for 2½ hours, then remove the lid and continue to cook, using a spoon to baste the lamb with the pan juices occasionally, until the lamb is golden on top and the meat is very tender, 1 to 1½ hours more. Remove from the oven, cover, and set aside to rest for 10 minutes before serving.

note | One of Richard Olney's many very excellent recipes calls for cooks to toss the garlic slices in a mixture of finely chopped herbs before inserting them into cuts of meat. He wrote that into a recipe for daube, but doing that here is awesome too, if a bit more time intensive. Joann has had and loved this recipe both ways, so take it or leave it as you please.

TO CONTINUE

WHEAT + PASTA

Sandwiches for "Hiking"

PAN BAGNAT

There are sandwiches for immediate consumption, and there are sandwiches to be made ahead of time. Pan bagnat, sandwich of the Côte d'Azur, is the latter. The longer the assembled sandwich sits (up to a whole day or so) the more flavorful it becomes. Layer the sandwiches the night before or the morning of and pack alongside other "hiking" essentials. Or be like me and call the stroll down to the beach a hike and reason enough for a sandwich. At Chez Josy, a seasonal shack on Plage de la Salis in Antibes—which is a superlative place to "hike" to eat a solid pan bagnat—they offer anchovies as optional. That's a yes for me, but as ever, as you like it.

Makes 4 sandwiches

2 medium ripe tomatoes, cut crosswise into ¼-inch [6 mm] slices

Fine sea salt

¼ cup [60 ml] red wine vinegar

2 teaspoons Dijon mustard

½ small red onion, finely chopped

Freshly ground black pepper

8 small radishes, finely chopped

1 small seedless cucumber or ½ large cucumber, peeled, seeded, and finely chopped

½ cup [120 ml] extra-virgin olive oil

2 baguettes or 4 large, round, crusty bread rolls, halved lengthwise

Two 5- to 6-ounce [140 to 170 g] jars tuna packed in olive oil, drained

¼ cup [40 g] Niçoise olives, pitted (or larger black olives, such as Kalamata, pitted and halved)

4 large hard-boiled eggs, peeled and thinly sliced lengthwise (see Note, page 208)

8 to 12 oil-cured anchovies, drained, if desired

Line a baking sheet with paper towels. Season the tomato slices with salt and place the tomatoes in a single layer on the prepared baking sheet. Let drain for 15 to 20 minutes.

In a medium bowl, whisk together the vinegar and mustard. Add the red onion, season with salt and pepper, and let sit for 10 minutes. Add the radishes, cucumber, and ¼ cup [60 ml] of the olive oil and stir to combine. Adjust the seasoning as needed.

Slice the baguettes in half lengthwise. Scoop out some of the insides from the center of each of the bread halves, discarding or reserving for another use. Drizzle each cut side of the bread with the remaining ¼ cup [60 ml] olive oil and season with salt and pepper.

Layer the tomatoes evenly across the bottom halves of the bread. Transfer the tuna to a small bowl and smash with a fork, then spread evenly over the tomatoes. Spoon the onion-radish-cucumber mixture over the tuna, then layer the olives, egg slices, and anchovies (if using) on top. Season with salt and pepper, then place the top halves of the bread on top, pressing down lightly. Wrap each sandwich tightly in plastic wrap or reusable beeswax wrap and place on a baking sheet. Place a heavy-bottomed pan or cast-iron skillet on top to weigh them down. Rest in the refrigerator for at least 2 hours, and up to overnight. Eat at room temperature.

The Pasta I Crave Every Time I'm near the Sea

At the country's most southeastern edge, Italy spills into France. On one side, the small, brightly hued city of Menton, rightly boastful of its lemons and more than 316 days of sunshine a year. A small sign, a dashed line on the map, and you're in Liguria. Borders, as we know, are constructs. Regardless, on either side, you're never far from the sea, and pasta abounds.

Serves 6 to 8

¾ cup [45 g] coarse, day-old bread crumbs

5 tablespoons [75 ml] extra-virgin olive oil

1 fennel bulb, bulb very thinly sliced and fronds finely chopped

1 lemon, zested and juiced

Fine sea salt

Freshly ground black pepper

4 shallots, thinly sliced

4 garlic cloves, thinly sliced

Red pepper flakes

1 pound [455 g] dried pasta, such as bucatini, spaghetti, or linguine

4 tablespoons [55 g] unsalted European butter, at room temperature

Pinch saffron threads, gently crushed with your fingertips or with a mortar and pestle

2 pounds [910 g] small clams, cleaned

1 cup Marinated Lemons (recipe follows)

1 cup [240 ml] dry white wine

Lemon wedges, for serving

In a small skillet over medium-high heat, toast the bread crumbs in 2 tablespoons of the olive oil until golden, 3 to 5 minutes. Stir in the fennel fronds and lemon zest and cook for 30 seconds more. Season with salt and pepper. Set aside.

In a large skillet over medium-high heat, heat the remaining 3 tablespoons of the olive oil until hot. Add the shallots and sliced fennel and cook, stirring often, until the shallots are translucent and the fennel is soft, 10 to 15 minutes. Season with salt and pepper, then add the garlic and red pepper flakes and continue to cook for 1 minute more.

While the shallots and fennel cook, add the pasta to a large pot of boiling salted water, stirring occasionally, until very al dente, 2 to 3 minutes fewer than the package directions (it should still have a slight crunch in the center). Drain, reserving 1 cup [240 ml] of the pasta cooking liquid.

Add 2 tablespoons of the butter and the saffron to the shallot-fennel mixture and stir until the butter is melted. Add the clams, tossing to combine, then add the marinated lemons and pour in the wine and ¼ cup [60 ml] of the reserved pasta cooking liquid. Cover the skillet and cook, shaking the pan occasionally, until the clams open, 4 to 6 minutes. Using tongs, pick out the clams and transfer to a large bowl, discarding any clams that have not opened. Loosely cover with foil to keep warm. CONTINUED

Add the pasta and another ¼ cup [60 ml] of the pasta cooking liquid to the skillet and stir to coat. Lower the heat to medium, add the remaining 2 tablespoons of butter, and continue to cook, stirring and adding more pasta cooking liquid as needed, until the sauce coats the pasta and the pasta is al dente, 3 to 4 minutes. Remove from the heat, return the clams to the pot, add the lemon juice, and toss to combine.

Transfer the pasta to a platter, sprinkle with the fennel frond–bread crumbs, and serve with additional lemon wedges.

Marinated Lemons

Makes about 2 cups [760 g]

In a small saucepan over medium heat, combine the oil, garlic, peppercorns, and bay leaves. Heat, stirring occasionally, until the garlic is golden around the edges, 5 to 7 minutes. Season with salt.

Add the lemon slices to a large glass storage jar and pour the warm garlic-oil mixture over the top. Let sit at room temperature overnight, then store in the refrigerator for up to 1 month.

1½ cups [360 ml] extra-virgin olive oil

4 garlic cloves, peeled and smashed

2 tablespoons pink or black peppercorns, lightly crushed

2 bay leaves

Fine sea salt

4 whole lemons, thinly sliced into ⅛-inch [4 mm] rounds (use standard lemons with thin rinds or Meyer lemons)

Pasta to Make When You're Not near the Sea (but Wish You Were)

No explanation necessary.

1 pound [455 g] dried long, flat pasta, such as tagliatelle, fettuccine, or pappardelle

6 tablespoons [90 ml] extra-virgin olive oil

6 garlic cloves, thinly sliced

6 oil-packed anchovy fillets, finely chopped

Two 5-ounce [140 g] tins sardines, preferably smoked, packed in oil, and coarsely chopped

2 tablespoons salted capers, rinsed, drained, and finely chopped

2 tablespoons finely chopped Preserved (Meyer) Lemons (page 81)

Red pepper flakes

6 tablespoons [85 g] unsalted European butter, at room temperature

¼ cup [60 ml] fresh lemon juice

1 cup [20 g] tightly packed fresh flat-leaf parsley leaves, finely chopped, plus more for serving

Flaky sea salt

Grated Parmigiano-Reggiano, for serving

Serves 6

Add the pasta to a large pot of boiling salted water, stirring occasionally, until very al dente, 2 to 3 minutes fewer than package directions (it should still have a slight crunch in the center). Drain, reserving 2 cups [480 ml] of the pasta cooking liquid.

While the pasta is cooking, in a large skillet set over medium heat, add the oil, garlic, and anchovies. Cook until the garlic is soft and pale golden but not browned, about 3 minutes. Add the sardines, capers, preserved lemons, and red pepper flakes and cook, stirring, for 1 minute more. Stir in the drained pasta and ¼ cup [60 ml] of the reserved pasta cooking liquid. Add the butter and continue to cook, stirring and adding more pasta cooking liquid as needed, until the sauce coats the pasta, about 4 minutes. Stir in the fresh lemon juice and parsley, season with salt to taste, and serve with Parmigiano-Reggiano and additional parsley.

Sugeli (c/o Madame Maffei)

The drive from Menton to the Roya Valley would take you, as it took me, over to Italy and back. En route, you would breathe salted, coastal air as you followed the Roya past waterfalls and up the mountain-edged road to La Brigue. The cross-border drive makes sense: La Brigue, along with neighboring Tende, were both Piedmontese territories until 1947, and the local dialect, Brigasque, has links to both the Genoese and Occitan languages.

I drove up for the day to learn to make sugeli, a traditional fresh pasta of the region, from one of the few women still making it today. This is Madame Maffei's recipe, shared in bits while she taught me and a handful of children from La Brigue and neighboring villages how to use our thumbs to shape the dough into small, ridged discs. Similar in shape to Italy's orecchiette, the fresh pasta is traditionally served—as part of cucina bianca, the region's culinary tradition—with nuts and brousse, a soft, thick sheep's milk cheese made locally. By the end of the afternoon, a clutch of (a few nearly perfect and many misshapen) sugeli at the ready, Mme Maffei assured me that, should I not have easy access to brousse back home, the fresh pasta goes just as nicely with everything from pistou (page 120) to ragù to gorgonzola sauce.

Serves 6 to 8

Spoon the flour into a pile on a wooden work surface. Using your hands, create a well in the center of the flour and carefully add the oil, salt, and 1¼ cups [300 ml] of room-temperature water to the center of the well. Use your hands to gently and gradually mix in the flour, working the dough to bring it into a shaggy ball. Knead until a very smooth dough forms and is no longer sticky, about 15 minutes, then shape the dough into a round and place a large bowl over the top (see Note). Set aside for 1 hour.

Lightly flour a wooden work surface and sheet pan. Use a dough cutter or knife to cut out a small piece of dough—re-covering the remaining dough ball with the

2 cups plus 2 tablespoons [310 g] all-purpose flour, plus more for dusting

3 tablespoons vegetable oil

Pinch fine sea salt

bowl. Use your hands to shape the dough into a large rope. Place your fingertips in the center of the rope and roll the dough back and forth, moving your hands outward and away from each other toward the end of the rope. Continue this motion until you create a rope about ¾ inch [2 cm] in diameter. (If the rope gets too long, simply cut it in half and roll the halves out separately.) Cut the dough into ¾-inch [2 cm] cubes.

On the very lightly floured work surface, use your thumb to firmly press and roll each piece of dough away from you, pressing firmly enough to form folds in the center but not so hard that you tear the dough. Pick up the sugeli and gently use your thumb to turn it inside out so a little dome—or hat—forms. Place in a single layer on the floured sheet pan and repeat with the remaining dough.

Let the formed pasta rest for 1 to 2 hours at room temperature (it should just hold its shape when handling).

To cook the pasta, working in small batches, add the sugeli to a large pot of boiling salted water. Cook just until the pasta rises to the surface, then remove with a slotted spoon. Transfer to a warm serving bowl and repeat until all the pasta is cooked. Once all the pasta is cooked, reserve 1 cup [240 ml] of the pasta cooking liquid. Add whatever sauce you're using to the pasta along with ¼ cup [60 ml] of the pasta cooking liquid. Toss vigorously to combine and serve immediately.

note | Mme Maffei insists that it is very important that les pâtes ne prennent pas l'air (the pasta dough isn't exposed to the air), which causes it to harden and thus makes the shaping of sugeli much more complicated. Keep any dough you're not using under an overturned bowl.

Pâtes au Pistou

A simple, fresh combination of garlic, basil, and olive oil, pistou—Provence's pine nut–less pesto analogue—brightens everything it touches. Drizzled over tomatoes (see page 167), stuffed into fish (see page 119) and, right here on this very page, tossed, green on green, Niçoise-style, with spinach pasta. It also freezes really nicely, so do that too.

Serves 4 to 6

To make the pistou: If you are making the pistou with a mortar and pestle: Place the garlic and salt in a mortar and grind until a paste forms. Add the basil leaves by the handful and pound them, scraping the sides of the mortar often, until they are almost smooth and all the basil is incorporated. Slowly add the oil, 1 tablespoon at a time, smashing until it's all combined. Stir in the cheeses and season with salt to taste.

If you are making the pistou with a blender: Place the garlic cloves in the blender and pulse until roughly chopped. Add the salt and the basil and pulse, scraping down the sides of the blender often, until the paste is nearly smooth. With the blender running, slowly pour in the oil until it's all combined. Stir in the cheeses and season with salt to taste.

To make the pasta: Add the pasta to a large pot of boiling salted water and cook, stirring occasionally, according to the package instructions if using dry pasta or 2 to 4 minutes if using fresh pasta. Drain, reserving 2 cups [480 ml] of the pasta cooking liquid.

Warm a large serving bowl and add the butter and pistou to the bowl. Add the hot pasta and ¼ cup [60 ml] pasta cooking liquid. Toss vigorously to combine, adding more pasta cooking water as needed, and serve immediately with more Parmigiano-Reggiano, if desired. CONTINUED

PISTOU

2 garlic cloves

½ teaspoon flaky sea salt, plus more to taste

3 cups [75 g] basil leaves

⅓ cup [80 ml] extra-virgin olive oil

2 tablespoons finely grated Emmental cheese

1 tablespoon finely grated Parmigiano-Reggiano cheese, plus more for serving if desired

PÂTES

1 pound [455 g] store-bought fresh or dried long, flat pasta, such as tagliatelle, fettuccine, or pappardelle, preferably spinach or homemade (see Note)

4 tablespoons [55 g] unsalted European butter

note | If you want to make your own fresh spinach pasta, steam or sauté about **5 cups [100 g] of baby spinach** until just wilted. Remove the spinach from the pan and spread out in a single layer on a clean dish towel. When the spinach is cool, use your hands to squeeze the leaves, one handful at a time, and discard the excess water. Roughly chop, then add to a blender or food processor with **2 cups [50 g] of fresh basil (or flat-leaf parsley)**. Pulse until the mixture is finely chopped, then add **2 large eggs**, **1 large egg yolk**, and **½ teaspoon fine sea salt**. Purée until a smooth mixture forms.

In the center of a clean work surface, add **2 cups [280 g] of all-purpose flour** in a large pile. Use your hands to create a well in the center and add the spinach-egg mixture. Use a fork to slowly incorporate the flour, starting at the inner rim and working your way out until a shaggy dough forms. Switch to using your hands and continue to mix until the dough forms. If the dough looks dry, add a teaspoon of very cold water. If the dough looks wet, add a little flour. Dust the surface with a bit more flour as needed and knead the dough until it is smooth (this should take a few minutes). Form into a ball, flatten into a 1-inch [2.5 cm] disc, and wrap in plastic wrap. Set aside at room temperature for 1 hour (and up to 4 hours).

When you are ready to roll your pasta, dust two baking sheets lightly with flour.

If you are rolling out your dough using a machine:
Unwrap the dough and divide it into four pieces. Rewrap
three of the pieces and flatten the remaining piece into a flat
oval about the width of your pasta machine. Set the rollers
to the widest (thickest) setting, dust the dough very lightly
with flour, and pass it through the rollers. Fold the dough
into thirds like a letter (again, it should be about the width
of your pasta machine) and pass the dough through a second
time. Repeat one or two more times on the same setting. At
this point, the dough should be smooth. Reduce the setting
and lightly dust both sides of the dough with flour. Roll the
dough through each of the settings twice, continuing until
the pasta is about $1/16$-inch [2 mm] thick (you'll stop rolling
when the dough is about two or three settings thicker than
the thinnest one on your roller). Cut the long pasta sheet
into shorter sheets, each 10 to 12 inches [25 to 30.5 cm]
long. Dust lightly with all-purpose flour or semolina flour
and stack on the prepared baking sheets. Cover with a
clean kitchen towel and repeat with the remaining dough
quarters.

If you are rolling out the dough by hand: Cut the
refrigerated disc of dough into two pieces and roll them out,
one at a time, on a lightly floured surface. It's not hard but
it does require patience to get them $1/16$-inch [2 mm] thick.

Cut the pasta sheets into $1/2$- to $3/4$-inch [12 mm to
2 cm] wide noodles and gently fluff and spread them onto
an all purpose— or semolina-dusted baking sheet. Cover
with a clean kitchen towel until ready to cook.

TO CONTINUE

VEGETABLES

How to Serve Perfect In-Season Tomatoes
(+ Anchovy Aïoli)

Ever make aïoli in a hotel room and then slice three pounds of peak-season tomatoes on an uneven rock wearing a hat you can barely see around on a public beach in Marseille? Until I dreamed up the idea for this image, me neither. Messy business, turns out. Also turns out, a very satisfying post-shoot, water-side meal. Skip the seaside cutting board, keep the peak-season tomatoes. Once you hit indoor weather, make Tomates à la Provençale, or How to Serve Perfect Out-of-Season Tomatoes (page 165).

3 pounds [1.4 kg] large, ripe heirloom tomatoes, stems removed

Flaky sea salt

Anchovy Aïoli (recipe follows)

8 to 12 whole anchovies packed in oil, if desired

Freshly ground black pepper

Serves 6

Use a sharp knife to slice the tomatoes crosswise into ½-inch [12 mm] rounds. Arrange the slices on a serving platter in a single layer and season lightly with salt. Spoon the anchovy aïoli over the top and top with anchovies (if using). Finish with pepper and serve.

Anchovy Aïoli

2 large egg yolks

1 teaspoon Dijon mustard

1 to 2 small garlic cloves, grated on a Microplane

¼ cup [60 ml] grapeseed or canola oil

½ cup [120 ml] extra-virgin olive oil

2 tablespoons fresh lemon juice

4 anchovies, finely chopped

½ teaspoon freshly ground black pepper

Hot sauce, if desired

Fine sea salt, if desired

Makes about 1 cup [240 ml]

In a medium bowl, whisk together the egg yolks, mustard, and garlic. Whisking constantly, add the grapeseed oil drop by drop until the mixture thickens. Continuing to whisk, pour in the olive oil in a slow, steady stream, then add the lemon juice in 1-teaspoon increments, whisking constantly. The aïoli mixture should be pale yellow and thick. Stir in the anchovies, black pepper, and hot sauce (if using). Taste for seasoning and add salt, if needed. CONTINUED

note | If you run out of anchovies (or simply don't want them), swap in finely chopped preserved lemons or capers or cornichons or lemon zest or a few dashes of something with spice.

note | Should you, say, find yourself in a seaside hotel room without a bowl and whisk and fresh eggs but are still determined to make this recipe (or another recipe in this book that deploys aïoli), you can stir fresh lemon juice and finely chopped garlic into GOOD store-bought mayo and use that instead. Just, s'il te plaît, don't call it aïoli and also please know that while I will always prefer a from-scratch aïoli to a hacked mayo, sometimes you make do with what you have.

How to Serve Perfect Out-of-Season Tomatoes

TOMATES À LA PROVENÇALE

When it's not summer, but you need summer, this is the one. While not traditional, I add a crumble of fresh chèvre to my Tomates à la Provençale because cheese. If you prefer to stay true to the classic or have a vegan friend coming to dinner, feel free to leave it off. You can always make Pink Peppercorn Marinated Chèvre (page 59) to start.

Serves 6 to 8

Line a baking sheet with paper towels. Slice the tops of the tomatoes off crosswise and, working over a bowl or the sink, use a spoon to gently scoop out the seeds and remove excess juice, taking care to leave the tomatoes' shapes intact. Season with salt and place the tomatoes upside down on the prepared baking sheet for at least 30 minutes and up to 1 hour.

Preheat the oven to 400°F [200°C]. Drizzle an ovenproof baking dish with 1 tablespoon of the olive oil and arrange the tomatoes cut sides up in the dish.

In a medium bowl, combine the garlic, parsley, herbes de Provence, and bread crumbs. Season with salt and pepper.

Crumble the chèvre and divide evenly among the tomatoes. Season with salt and pepper, then sprinkle the bread crumb mixture evenly over the top. Drizzle with the remaining 2 tablespoons of olive oil and place in the oven. Bake until the topping is golden brown and the tomatoes are soft and tender but keep their shape, about 15 minutes. Serve warm or at room temperature.

10 medium, thick-skinned greenhouse tomatoes

Fine sea salt

3 tablespoons extra-virgin olive oil

3 garlic cloves, finely chopped

½ bunch fresh flat-leaf parsley, finely chopped

1 teaspoon herbes de Provence (see Note, page 59)

¾ cup [45 g] coarse, day-old bread crumbs

Freshly ground black pepper

4 ounces [115 g] fresh chèvre

Cherry Tomatoes with Pistou

Sometimes when we write cookbooks, it's too easy to fall into the old ways. When you've read countless great ones, you get to know how they're written, how they're organized and shot, and how the headnote for a recipe like this would be like…"This may initially read as a side dish—and it is particularly good on the table alongside Market Day Roast Chicken + Potatoes (page 95), Whole Roasted Fish (page 119), or Lamb for Joann (page 137)—but if you're bold enough, serve this one up as a main course and change people's minds about what a cherry tomato can be!"

But, like, what even *is* a side dish? Is that even how we eat anymore? Here's what I know chère lectrice: These tomatoes are really very good and would be great alongside a bunch of other things in this book or not.

Serves 6

To roast the red peppers, preheat the oven to 400°F [200°C] and arrange one oven rack near the top of the oven and the other in the middle of the oven. Place the bell peppers on a baking sheet and drizzle with 1 tablespoon of the olive oil. Use your hands to rub the oil over the peppers.

Place the peppers on the top rack and roast for 25 minutes then flip the peppers over with tongs and continue roasting until the peppers are charred all over and very soft, about 15 minutes more.

While the peppers are roasting, combine the cherry tomatoes and the remaining 2 tablespoons of olive oil on a second baking sheet. Season with salt and roast until the tomatoes are very soft and beginning to burst, 20 to 30 minutes.

Transfer the peppers to a heatproof bowl, cover with a plate, and set aside to cool to room temperature. Once the peppers are cooled, remove the skins and discard the stems and seeds. Quarter the peppers and transfer to a serving platter along with the tomatoes. Drizzle with the pistou, season with salt, and serve. Leftovers will keep, tightly covered and refrigerated, for up to 3 days.

4 red bell peppers

3 tablespoons extra-virgin olive oil

6 cups [960 g] cherry tomatoes

Flaky sea salt

½ cup [120 ml] A Very Classic Pistou (page 120)

Haricots Verts with Shallots, Capers, Preserved Lemon

At marchés across Provence, haricots verts pile high from July to September. After spending half the summer grabbing them by the handful, barely blanching them (harvested young, they're a dream to cook, by which I mean they take barely any time), and then tossing the long, thin, tender beans with salted butter and herbs—a classic, delicate side—I get bored and want more. Enter this shallot, garlic, caper, preserved lemon, and harissa combination.

Serves 6

1¼ pounds [570 g] haricots verts or green beans, trimmed

5 tablespoons [75 ml] extra-virgin olive oil

4 medium shallots, thinly sliced into rounds

2 garlic cloves, finely chopped

¼ cup [30 g] salted capers, soaked, rinsed, drained, and coarsely chopped

2 tablespoons finely chopped Preserved (Meyer) Lemons (page 81) or store-bought preserved lemons

2 tablespoons red or white wine vinegar

1 to 2 tablespoons harissa

Flaky sea salt

Bring a large pot of salted water to a boil. Add the haricots verts and cook until bright green and crisp-tender, 2 minutes. Drain the beans and set aside.

Set a large skillet over medium heat and add 4 tablespoons [60 ml] of the oil. Once the oil is hot, add the shallots and cook, stirring frequently, until the shallots are tender and beginning to brown, about 5 minutes. Add the garlic and capers and cook for 1 minute. Stir in the preserved lemon, vinegar, and harissa. Add the beans and 2 tablespoons of water. Toss to coat the beans with the mixture and heat through, then transfer to a serving platter. Drizzle with the remaining 1 tablespoon of olive oil, season with salt, and serve warm or at room temperature.

note | Keep in mind that if you use shorter, thicker, heartier green beans rather than haricots verts (which, yes, means "green beans" in French) they'll take a little longer to cook.

Ratatouille

2 medium eggplants, (about 1¼ pounds [570 g]), cut into ¾-inch [2 cm] dice

2½ teaspoons fine sea salt, plus more for seasoning

½ cup plus 6 tablespoons [210 ml] extra-virgin olive oil, plus more for serving

2 medium white onions, cut into ¾-inch [2 cm] dice

3 medium zucchini, cut into ¾-inch [2 cm] dice

3 medium red sweet bell peppers, cut into ¾-inch [2 cm] dice

6 garlic cloves, finely chopped

3 tablespoons tomato paste

2 teaspoons honey, preferably lavender

3 medium beefsteak or heirloom tomatoes, cut into ¾-inch [2 cm] dice, or one 14-ounce [400 g] can plum tomatoes, coarsely chopped

4 sprigs fresh thyme

2 bay leaves

¼ cup [60 ml] dry white wine, rosé, or vermouth

If you take away one thing from this book, let it be this: Ratatouille takes time. Or rather, *good* ratatouille takes time. Sure, throw everything in the pan to cook all at once and you will quickly end up with a mediocre approximation. But along the way, the eggplant will have lost a bit of its eggplant-ness, the zucchini some of its zucchini-ness... you get it. To cook ratatouille's vegetables separately, each in its own bath of olive oil, before layering them together in a tangled jumble at the end, is time well spent. This recipe is inspired by two separate but memorable ratatouille—one ordered in Nice and eaten as a precarious yet functional car snack on the coastal drive to Saint-Tropez; the other ordered at a hotel, also on the coast between Nice and Saint-Tropez, with ridiculous views (and prices to match)—each made slightly sweeter, richer, and deeper in flavor with the additions of honey and tomato paste.

Serves 6

Add the diced eggplant to a colander and toss with the salt. Set aside to drain for 20 to 30 minutes, then, working in batches, pat the eggplant dry with paper towels.

While the eggplants are draining, set a large skillet over medium heat and add ¼ cup [60 ml] of the oil. Once the oil is hot, add the onions and cook, stirring occasionally, until the onions are very soft and lightly browned, 20 to 30 minutes. Season with salt and transfer the onions to a large bowl.

In the same pan, add another ¼ cup [60 ml] of the oil to the skillet. Add the eggplant and cook, stirring frequently, until the eggplant is golden on all sides and tender, 15 to 20 minutes. Transfer the eggplant to the bowl with the onions.

Add 2 tablespoons of the oil and the zucchini to the skillet. Cook for 5 minutes, stirring often, then season lightly with salt and continue to cook until the zucchini are browned and soft, 8 to 10 minutes. Transfer to the bowl with the onions and eggplant. CONTINUED

Again in the same skillet, add 2 tablespoons of the oil and the bell peppers and cook, stirring often, until the peppers are very tender, about 15 minutes. Transfer to the bowl.

Add the remaining 2 tablespoons of oil and the garlic to the skillet. Cook for 1 minute, then add the tomato paste and honey and cook, stirring, for 1 minute more. Add the tomatoes, thyme, and bay leaves and season with salt. Cook, stirring occasionally, until most of the liquid evaporates, about 15 minutes.

Stir in the wine and cook for 2 minutes, then return the rest of the vegetables to the skillet and continue to cook, stirring often, for another 15 minutes. Season with salt to taste, then remove from the heat. Remove and discard the thyme and bay leaves. Serve warm or at room temperature, finished with a final drizzle of olive oil. Ratatouille will keep, tightly covered and refrigerated, for up to 3 days.

note | If you have even more time, make ratatouille a day or two in advance and serve the next day to give the flavors even more time to deepen.

La Bohémienne

If you simply must visit the lavender fields of Provence, go in early to mid-July. There are plenty to drive by but if you prefer a stop, the Abbaye Notre-Dame de Sénanque faces a huge lavender field super close to the very pretty hilltop village of Gordes. While we're on the topic of seasonal purple things, you'll be there at the start of eggplant season, which means you should make la bohémienne. The recipe on page 173 involves cooking vegetables separately before combining them into a total-greater-than-sum-of-parts mélange. La bohémienne, or bóumiano in Provençal, drops the zucchini and peppers, adds anchovies, and you cook the mid- to late-summer garden trove of eggplant, tomato, and onion together long enough for the lines between vegetables to blur into a soft, silky, savory, stew-like riot, and that's good too.

Serves 6

Toss the diced eggplant with the salt. Transfer to a colander and set aside to drain for 20 to 30 minutes. Use paper towels to pat the eggplant dry.

Set a large skillet with a tight-fitting lid over medium heat and add 2 tablespoons of the oil. Add the onion and cook, stirring occasionally, until the onion is tender and translucent, about 10 minutes. Stir in the garlic and anchovies. Cook for 1 minute more, then add the remaining 6 tablespoons [90 ml] of oil and the eggplant to the pan. Cook, stirring frequently, for 10 minutes, then add the tomatoes, wine, bay leaves, and red pepper flakes (if using). Cover the pan, lower the heat to medium-low, and cook, stirring occasionally, for 1 hour.

After 1 hour, the eggplant should be tender and silky. Remove the lid and return to a simmer. Cook, stirring, for another 15 minutes until some of the liquid evaporates. Taste for seasoning and season with salt as needed. Serve warm or at room temperature. La Bohémienne will keep, tightly covered and refrigerated, for up to 3 days.

4 medium eggplants (about 2½ pounds [1.2 kg]), cut into ½-inch [12 mm] dice

1 tablespoon fine sea salt, plus more as needed

½ cup [120 ml] extra-virgin olive oil

1 large yellow onion, cut into ½-inch [12 mm] dice

4 garlic cloves, finely chopped

2 anchovies, finely chopped

2 pounds [910 kg] (about 6 medium) plum or heirloom tomatoes, cut into ½-inch [12 mm] dice

½ cup [120 ml] dry white wine

2 bay leaves

Red pepper flakes, if desired

Tian

Assembling a tian often occupies a slice of my afternoons in Provence. It's a mind-resetting culinary pause between lunch and apéro, with a background track of cicadas and, depending on if we're on holidays or not, keyboard percussion. It's meditative to stand alone in the kitchen, tucking slices of vegetables tightly together, alternating colors and textures in the baking dish, letting your mind wander.

Don't be too precious about the ingredient list; the beauty of a tian is that you can and should use whatever you find in the garden or at the market. Planted too much zucchini and can't shove any more off on your neighbors? Use extra zucchini. Add eggplant, skip the potatoes, sprinkle bread crumbs on top, throw a swipe of tomato sauce on the bottom of the dish. Any tian tastes best made a bit in advance and served at room temperature, so make it between emails or swims, letting it sit on the counter until dinner.

Serves 6

4 tablespoons [60 ml] extra-virgin olive oil

6 medium shallots, thinly sliced

3 garlic cloves, thinly sliced

2 sprigs fresh thyme

Pinch red pepper flakes, if desired

Fine sea salt

Freshly ground black pepper

2 tablespoons dry white wine or vermouth

3 or 4 medium zucchini or summer squash, sliced into ¼-inch [6 mm] thick rounds

3 or 4 medium Yukon gold potatoes, sliced into ¼-inch [6 mm] thick rounds

6 to 8 medium, ripe tomatoes, sliced into ¼-inch [6 mm] thick rounds

Preheat the oven to 400°F [200°C].

In a large skillet over medium heat, add 2 tablespoons of the oil. When the oil is hot, add the shallots and cook, stirring often, until they are tender and translucent, about 10 minutes. Add the garlic, thyme, and red pepper flakes (if using). Season with salt and pepper and continue to cook for 1 minute more. Pour in the wine and use a wooden spoon to scrape up any bits stuck to the bottom of the pan. Cook until the liquid evaporates, about 1 minute, then transfer the shallot-garlic mixture to a 9-by-13-inch [23 by 33 cm] baking dish, discarding the thyme sprigs.

Alternate adding the zucchini, potatoes, and tomatoes to the baking dish in one layer, overlapping the slices, and packing the rows tightly together. Season with salt and pepper and drizzle with the remaining 2 tablespoons of oil.

Bake until the vegetables are tender and lightly browned, 35 to 40 minutes. Serve warm or at room temperature. Tian will keep, tightly covered and refrigerated, for up to 3 days.

Aïoli, Petit to Monstre

2 large egg yolks

¼ cup [60 ml] grapeseed or canola oil

½ cup [120 ml] extra-virgin olive oil

1 to 2 tablespoons fresh lemon juice

2 small garlic cloves, grated on a Microplane

Fine sea salt

SOME (OR ALL) OF THE FOLLOWING DEPENDING ON THE SIZE AND SCALE OF YOUR AÏOLI:

Tiny boiled potatoes

Hard- or soft-boiled eggs (see page 208)

Radishes

Blanched green beans

Small ripe tomatoes, sliced or quartered

Small heads of lettuce, quartered

Other seasonal vegetables

Cooked chickpeas (see page 211)

Poached salt cod

Steamed mussels (see Note, page 107)

Crusty bread

Since meeting my partner, my aïoli consumption—already high, mind you—has dramatically increased. The main reason for this is that she makes the aïoli. Oil and eggs, magicked one golden drop at a time into glossy, garlicky, emulsified perfection in which to dip all manner of things, is a task best suited to those with excess patience and arm strength. Naturally, the best of our aïolis have happened in Provence, where aïoli is woven into life. Here, *aïoli* refers to both sauce and meal and spans in size from pétit to grande to monstre.

A few tiny potatoes, boiled eggs, maybe some radishes, and crusty bread make a fine **pétit aïoli** for two. Adding poached salt cod, blanched green beans, small ripe tomatoes, small quartered heads of lettuce, and other seasonal vegetables makes it **grande**—often, ever-charmingly, served for a Provençal Friday lunch. All the above plus tiny snails, chickpeas, shellfish, and any and all vegetables found at the market elevates it to **monstre**. Across the region, this monster of an aïoli may manifest as an entire village coming together to partake. Choose your size according to your needs, remembering that the centerpiece of any size aïoli is the aïoli itself—the very sun of the Provençal universe.

Makes about 1 cup [240 ml] aïoli

To make the aïoli: In a medium bowl, whisk the egg yolks. Whisking constantly, add the grapeseed oil drop by drop until the mixture thickens. Continuing to whisk constantly, pour in the remainder of the grapeseed oil and the olive oil in a slow, steady stream. Add the lemon juice in 1 teaspoon increments, whisking constantly. The aïoli mixture should be pale yellow and thick. Stir in the garlic, season with salt, and transfer to a serving bowl. Serve as many or as few of your chosen vegetables, seafood, and bread to make your aïoli petit, grand, or monstre. CONTINUED *note* | For ease, especially if you're planning something on the larger aïoli spectrum, prepare everything in advance. Cut what needs to be cut, blanch what needs to be blanched, poach what needs to be poached, ask your partner or friend or relative to whisk as much aïoli as needs to be whisked, and keep it all in the refrigerator to be assembled the next day.

note to relever l'aïoli | Should your aïoli break—it happens to us all—whisk another egg yolk with a tiny amount of lemon juice in a new bowl and start whisking in the broken aïoli, very slowly, starting drop by drop and increasing only as the emulsion feels sturdy.

EL ST HUB
HOTEL RESTAURANT
BAR À VINS
PETITS
RODUCTEURS
CAFÉ ARTISANAL
PÂTISSERIES
MAISON

Sauce Gribiche
(and Something to Put It On)

I think of sauce gribiche as vinaigrette with more texture. Rich and acidic, soft and crunchy, it's studded with capers and cornichons and eggs and can be spooned over just about anything. I especially like it with asparagus (see Note) but small boiled potatoes, radishes, leftover cold meats (page 137 or page 95), or even as a nouveau take on wedge salad all suit just fine. Judith Jones, arbiter of extremely good taste from Child to Hazan to Jaffrey to Lewis to Roden to Cunningham, wrote in her memoir that she preferred her eggs to be very finely chopped. I like mine with a little body, but you chop them as finely, or less finely, as you like.

Makes 1¼ cups [300 ml]

In a medium bowl, whisk together the mustard and vinegar. Slowly add the oil, whisking until emulsified; stir in the capers, cornichons, eggs, and parsley. Season with salt and pepper. Gribiche will keep, tightly covered and refrigerated, for up to 3 days.

note to blanch asparagus | Bring a pot of salted water to a boil. Add cleaned and trimmed asparagus and cook until bright green and crisp tender, 2½ to 4 minutes depending on the size of your asparagus. Drain and transfer the asparagus to a platter. Squeeze a half a lemon over the top, drizzle with very good olive oil, and season with salt.

2 tablespoons Dijon mustard

2 tablespoons white wine vinegar

¼ cup [60 ml] extra-virgin olive oil

2 tablespoons capers, finely chopped

5 to 8 cornichons, finely chopped

2 large hard-boiled eggs (see Note, page 208), chopped

3 tablespoons finely chopped fresh flat-leaf parsley

Fine sea salt

Freshly ground black pepper

Carottes Rosés

I started making this take on the very classic French carottes râpées while on holiday in a rented kitchen in Cavaillon. Armed with a peeler but no grater (and glass cutting boards, shudder), the carrots in this version are long and thin. To further depart from tradition, rather than a simple toss with oil and lemon juice, I pour a mixture of hot vinegar and rosé wine over the top, essentially quickly and lightly pickling the bright orange ribbons. When carottes rosés make it to the table, however, they serve the very same fresh, clean, hit-of-vitamin-C purpose as their grated forebearers.

Serves 6

Use a peeler to shave the carrots into long, thin strips and place in a large, heatproof bowl.

In a medium saucepan over medium-high heat, add ⅓ cup [80 ml] of the water, the vinegar, rosé, honey, garlic, parsley, bay leaf, and salt and bring to a boil, stirring to dissolve the honey and salt. Lower the heat and simmer for 5 minutes. Remove the pan from the heat, whisk in the olive oil and mustard, then pour the hot liquid over the carrots, toss to coat, and set aside to marinate for at least 1 hour.

Serve at room temperature. Carottes rosés can be made up to 4 hours in advance and are best eaten the day they are made.

note | Should you want to make this without alcohol, simply add a bit more water and cider vinegar.

2 pounds [910 g] carrots

⅓ cup [80 ml] cider vinegar

⅓ cup [80 ml] dry rosé wine

2 teaspoons honey, preferably lavender

1 small garlic clove, lightly crushed

4 sprigs parsley

1 bay leaf

1 teaspoon fine sea salt

¼ cup [60 ml] extra-virgin olive oil

1 teaspoon Dijon mustard

Olive Oil–Braised Carrots + Chickpeas

Chickpeas cooked in tomato sauce are ubiquitous across Provence, and I ate them quite a bit when I was recovering from long COVID, which means, of course, that I can never eat them again. I think I prefer mine braised in olive oil anyhow. Cooked alongside carrots, they take on that mellow sweetness, turning silky-soft, creamy, and complex with a long, slow simmer.

Serves 6 to 8

In a large Dutch oven or pot with a lid over medium heat, add the carrots, chickpeas, lemon slices, olive oil, wine, garlic, anchovies, capers, thyme, and bay leaf. Season with salt and pepper. Bring to a gentle simmer, tossing to coat the vegetables in the liquid, then cover the pot and cook until the carrots and chickpeas are very soft and tender, 30 to 40 minutes, tossing about halfway through cooking. Set aside to cool slightly, then remove and discard the thyme sprigs and bay leaf. Serve warm or at room temperature.

Olive oil–braised carrots + chickpeas can be made up to 4 hours in advance and left at room temperature, or refrigerated and stored in an airtight container for up to 3 days in advance. Gently reheat before serving.

note | If you like spice (I do), add a pinch of red pepper flakes while the carrots and chickpeas cook, or serve the finished dish with a dollop of harissa.

2 pounds [910 g] carrots, peeled and halved lengthwise, larger carrots quartered

One 15-ounce [430 g] can chickpeas

1 small, thin-skinned lemon, thinly sliced and seeds discarded

⅔ cup [160 ml] extra-virgin olive oil

⅓ cup [80 ml] dry white wine

3 garlic cloves, thinly sliced

3 anchovy fillets

2 tablespoons salted capers, soaked, rinsed, and drained

3 sprigs fresh thyme

1 bay leaf

Fine sea salt

Freshly ground black pepper

Salt + Vinegar Potatoes

Everyone knows that the best potato chips, forever and always, put it/them on my gravestone, are salt and vinegar. The sharper the vinegar, the better. Barring setting a family-size bag on the dinner table, make these.

Serves 6

In a large, heavy skillet or nonstick pan with a lid, add the olive oil and set over medium heat. When the oil is hot, add the potatoes, season with salt, and cook, stirring occasionally, until all the potatoes are deeply golden brown in parts, 12 to 15 minutes. Add the butter, 3 tablespoons of the vinegar, and ½ cup [120 ml] of water; lower the heat to low. Use a wooden spoon to gently scrape up any caramelized bits, then cover the pan and simmer until the potatoes are tender, caramelized, and easily pierced with a fork or paring knife, about 15 minutes.

Remove the lid, season with salt and pepper, and increase the heat to medium-high. Continue to cook, stirring, for 5 minutes more. Stir in the remaining 3 tablespoons of vinegar and transfer to a serving platter, sprinkle with salt, and serve immediately. Any leftover potatoes will keep, stored in an airtight container in the refrigerator, for up to 3 days (but are best eaten hot and immediately).

¼ cup [60 ml] extra-virgin olive oil

2½ pounds [1.2 kg] small new potatoes, washed, dried, and halved lengthwise

Flaky sea salt

2 tablespoons unsalted European butter, cut into small pieces

6 tablespoons [90 ml] apple cider vinegar

Freshly ground black pepper

Potatoes en Croûte de Sel Provençal

Cooking potatoes in salt insulates and seasons them in tandem, so by the time you bring the dish directly to the table to crack for your guests in true dinner-and-a-show fashion, the potatoes have gently cooked to dense, creamy, flawlessly salted perfection. Everyone should really be doing this more.

Serves 6

Preheat the oven to 400°F [200°C].

Remove the leaves from the thyme sprigs and finely chop. In a large bowl, combine the salt, thyme leaves, and peppercorns. Add about 1 cup [240 ml] of water and mix until the mixture is fragrant and resembles wet sand. Spread a third of the salt mixture onto the bottom of a shallow baking dish. Tuck the potatoes into the salt in an even layer, then add the remaining salt on top, using your hands to tightly pack the salt firmly, covering the potatoes completely. Tuck the bay leaves into the top layer of the salt.

Bake until a knife easily pierces the potatoes and the salt is hard to the touch, 40 to 50 minutes. To serve, use a serving spoon to crack the baked salt mixture and dig out the hot potatoes. Any leftover potatoes will keep, stored in an airtight container in the refrigerator, for up to 3 days (but are best eaten hot and immediately).

note | Instead of fresh thyme, you can use herbes de Provence (see Note, page 59) in this recipe.

8 sprigs fresh thyme

1½ pounds [680 g] kosher salt (about 4 cups)

1 tablespoon black or pink peppercorns

2 pounds [910 g] small waxy potatoes, washed and dried

2 bay leaves

French Fries

I'm willing to hear your arguments on this one, but for me, the fries, when done right, are the point. Everything else is garnish. Some garnishes I like: Moules in Aïoli (page 107) or Poisson Froid Mayonnaise (page 123) or Steak à la Beurre d'Anchois (page 135).

Serves 6 to 8

Add the potatoes to a large bowl and cover with cold water. Set aside to soak for 2 hours (or place in the refrigerator and soak overnight).

When you are ready to make the fries, line two baking sheets with paper towels. Drain the potatoes from the water and transfer to the baking sheets, blotting them dry as much as possible.

In a large Dutch oven or pot over high heat, add the oil and heat to 325°F [165°C]. Working in batches, cook the potatoes until soft but not brown, about 5 minutes per batch. Use a slotted spoon or spider to transfer each batch to fresh paper towels. When all the potatoes have been fried, increase the heat until the oil reaches 400°F [200°C]. Cook the potatoes in batches again, until golden and crisp, 2 to 3 minutes per batch. Transfer to fresh paper towels, season with salt, and serve immediately.

3 pounds [1.4 kg] russet potatoes, peeled and cut into ¼-inch [6 mm] thick sticks

6 to 8 cups [1.4 to 2 L] vegetable oil, for frying

Flaky sea salt

Crispy Mushrooms with Tapenade

Mushroom picking in Provence is a national sport: There are rules, a season, and a dedicated following. I consider my part in all this to be of the let-the-experts-do-the-foraging variety. I roast my (market or very, very trusted friend) haul in a hot hot oven and spoon Tapenade Noire ou Verte (page 48) over the top.

Serves 6

Preheat the oven to 425°F [220°C].

Divide the mushrooms between two rimmed baking sheets and drizzle with the olive oil. Add the thyme, season with salt and pepper, and toss gently to coat evenly. Spread the mushrooms in a single layer and roast until they are golden brown and the edges are crisp, tossing about halfway through, 25 to 30 minutes. Serve warm or at room temperature with tapenade.

2 pounds [910 g] mixed mushrooms, such as oyster, cremini, shiitake, or chanterelles, roughly chopped

½ cup [120 ml] olive oil

8 sprigs fresh thyme

Fine sea salt

Freshly ground black pepper

Tapenade Noire ou Verte (page 48)

Gazpacho para Ella

The French word for heat wave—*la canicule*—rolls off the tongue, a prettier way to announce an unpretty reality. In Provence, la canicule turns the already strong summer heat up to a simmer. It's too hot to think, too hot to stand, too hot to cook. During one such July moment in the Luberon Valley, my partner and I mustered the energy to get out of the pool and under the shade of Le Saint Hubert, a purple-shuttered restaurant owned by friends in the center of Saint-Saturnin-lès-Apt. Laila ordered gazpacho and hasn't stopped talking about it since. This is the version I make for her when Le Saint Hubert is out of reach.

Serves 4 | Makes about 5 cups [1.2 L]

In a large bowl, combine the heirloom tomatoes, melon, cucumbers, shallot, and garlic; season with salt. Toss to combine, then let sit at room temperature for 1 hour.

Transfer the mixture and any accumulated juices to a blender and blend until smooth. With the motor running, add the vinegar, then slowly drizzle in the olive oil. Add hot sauce and season with salt as needed. Refrigerate until chilled, at least 1 hour and up to overnight (or serve immediately).

When you're nearly ready to serve, in a medium bowl, toss the cherry tomatoes with salt and set aside for 10 minutes. Add cherry tomatoes to each bowl and top with about 1 cup [240 ml] of the gazpacho. Drizzle with olive oil and serve chilled. Gazpacho will keep, stored in an airtight container in the refrigerator, for 3 to 4 days.

2½ pounds [1.2 kg] small, ripe heirloom tomatoes

½ medium, ripe cantaloupe melon, rind and seeds discarded and flesh chopped

2 small seedless cucumbers, chopped

1 large shallot, chopped

1 to 2 garlic cloves

Flaky sea salt

2 tablespoons sherry or red wine vinegar

¼ cup [60 ml] extra-virgin olive oil, plus more for serving

Hot sauce, to taste

4 cups [640 g] ripe cherry tomatoes, halved

TO CONTINUE

SALADS

OPPOSITE:
The (Chickpea) Picnic Salad **209**

Herbed Salade Verte

HERBED VINAIGRETTE

2 medium shallots, finely chopped

2 tablespoons red wine vinegar

2 tablespoons fresh lemon juice

Fine sea salt

1 tablespoon grainy mustard

1 to 2 teaspoons honey, preferably lavender

¾ cup [180 ml] extra-virgin olive oil

2 cups [24 g] (about ½ bunch) fresh flat-leaf parsley leaves, finely chopped

1 cup [12 g] (about ½ bunch) fresh mint leaves, finely chopped

1 cup [12 g] (about ½ bunch) fresh dill or fennel fronds, coarsely chopped

½ cup [15 g] coarsely chopped chives

Freshly ground black pepper

SALADE VERTE

1 medium head leafy greens, torn

2 cups [24 g] (about ½ bunch) fresh flat-leaf parsley leaves

1 cup [12 g] (about ½ bunch) fresh mint leaves

1 cup [12 g] (about ½ bunch) fresh dill or fennel fronds

½ cup [15 g] coarsely chopped chives

Flaky sea salt

Freshly ground black pepper

The current herb garden at La Pitchoune, Julia Child's former Provençal home, is mere steps from the iconic pegboarded kitchen. Neatly planted rows, made unruly with a bounty of flourishing parsley, thyme, rosemary, sage, chervil, basil, no fewer than four varieties of mint, tarragon, and dill, all ready to be snipped with scissors grabbed from their designated outline on the way out the door. This salad, best made in close proximity to a garden or market bursting with tufts of perky, green herbs, disperses them in parts: finely chopped in the vinaigrette as well as left whole as part of the salad's bounty of greens.

Serves 6

To make the vinaigrette: In a resealable jar, combine the shallots, vinegar, and lemon juice. Season with fine sea salt, stir to combine, and let sit for at least 15 minutes. Add the mustard and honey, then pour in the oil, cover the jar tightly with a lid, and shake to emulsify. Stir in the chopped parsley, mint, dill, and chives and season with fine sea salt and pepper. The vinaigrette will keep, stored in an airtight container in the refrigerator, for up to 3 days.

   To make the salad: Transfer the vinaigrette to a large salad bowl. Add the greens, parsley, mint, dill, and chives and toss to coat. Season with flaky sea salt and pepper. Serve immediately.

note | Sometimes I add chopped green olives or cornichons to this vinaigrette. If you'd like to do that sometimes too, stir them in when you add the chopped herbs.

Greens with Tomato Vinaigrette

Make this when the tomatoes at the market feel almost too heavy in your hand, right around the time you're making How to Serve Perfect In-Season Tomatoes (page 161).

Serves 6

To make the vinaigrette: In a resealable jar, combine the shallots and vinegar. Season with fine sea salt and pepper, stir to combine, and let sit for at least 15 minutes.

Set a fine-mesh sieve over a mixing bowl and squeeze the tomato halves into the sieve, pressing on the solids to extract all the liquid. You should get about ½ cup [120 ml] of tomato juice. Discard the tomato halves.

Add the tomato juice, mustard, honey, and hot sauce (if using) to the jar and stir to combine. Pour in the oil, cover the jar tightly with a lid, and shake to emulsify. Season with fine sea salt and pepper. You should have about 1 cup [240 ml] of vinaigrette. The vinaigrette will keep, stored in an airtight container in the refrigerator, for 2 to 3 days.

To make the salad: Transfer some of the vinaigrette to a large salad bowl. Add the greens and toss to coat. Sprinkle with flaky sea salt and serve immediately with extra vinaigrette on the side.

VINAIGRETTE

1 large or 2 small shallots, thinly sliced into rounds

2 tablespoons red wine vinegar

Fine sea salt

Freshly ground black pepper

1 pound [455 g] ripe heirloom tomatoes (about 3 medium), halved crosswise

2 tablespoons Dijon mustard

1 teaspoon honey, preferably lavender

Hot sauce, if desired

½ cup [120 ml] extra-virgin olive oil

SALAD

1 large head leafy greens, torn

Flaky sea salt

204

Traditional Salade Niçoise + Not Traditional Salade Niçoise

Everyone, in and very far out of Nice, has an opinion of what does or does not belong in salade Niçoise. Some say the only thing in the salade that should be cooked are the eggs (a.k.a. no blanched green beans, no boiled potatoes). Others claim there should absolutely always be anchovies or canned tuna but never both. Still others: no vinegar in a Niçoise, no mustard, no lettuce. Some include one or more of the following: cucumbers, fava beans, thinly sliced raw artichokes, radishes, raw bell peppers, basil. Most seem to agree that a salade Niçoise should be presented as a salade composée (meaning, instead of tossing the ingredients all together in the bowl, they are composed, side by side) and contain small, unpitted olives from Nice.

You gotta do what feels right for you when that craving hits, but Niçoise can be truly bad, so use one of the following, depending on how traditional the vibes.

Traditional Salade Niçoise

1 garlic clove, halved

2 pounds [910 g] ripe tomatoes, cut into wedges

Flaky sea salt

½ cup [120 ml] extra-virgin olive oil

6 large eggs, hard boiled (see Note)

3 spring onions or scallions, white and light green parts only, thinly sliced

¾ cup [120 g] Niçoise olives

12 to 18 whole anchovies packed in oil (2 or 3 per person) OR two 6-ounce [170 g] cans tuna packed in olive oil, drained

Serves 6

Rub the inside of a large, shallow serving bowl or platter with the cut half of the garlic. Arrange the tomatoes on the platter and season lightly with salt. Let sit for 10 minutes, then drizzle the tomatoes with ¼ cup [60 ml] of the olive oil. Halve the eggs lengthwise and season the cut side of the eggs lightly with salt. Arrange the eggs, spring onions, olives, and anchovies or tuna in separate piles on top of or next to the tomatoes. Drizzle with the remaining ¼ cup [60 ml] of olive oil and serve.

Not Traditional Salade Niçoise

VINAIGRETTE

1 small garlic clove, grated on a Microplane

3 tablespoons red wine vinegar

Fine sea salt

½ cup [120 ml] extra-virgin olive oil

½ cup [12.5 g] lightly packed fresh basil, very thinly sliced

Freshly ground black pepper

SALAD

8 ounces [230 g] ripe heirloom tomatoes, cut into wedges, or cherry tomatoes, halved

Flaky sea salt

8 ounces [230 g] haricots verts or green beans, trimmed

8 ounces [230 g] small waxy potatoes

3 to 4 cups [60 to 80 g] mesclun lettuce (or a mix of mâche, frisée, arugula, escarole, baby spinach, and/ or radicchio)

6 large eggs, soft boiled (see Note)

1 small seedless cucumber, thinly sliced on the bias

6 to 8 small radishes, thinly sliced into rounds

2 spring onions or scallions, white and light green parts only, thinly sliced

Two 6-ounce [170 g] cans tuna packed in olive oil, drained

12 whole anchovies packed in oil

½ cup [80 g] Niçoise olives

Serves 6

To make the vinaigrette: In a small bowl, combine the garlic and red wine vinegar. Season with fine sea salt and let sit for 5 minutes. Slowly add the oil, whisking until the vinaigrette is emulsified; stir in the basil and season with fine sea salt and pepper. You should have about ¾ cup [180 ml].

To make the salad: In a medium bowl, add the tomatoes and season lightly with flaky sea salt. Set aside while you make the haricots verts and potatoes.

Line a baking sheet with a kitchen towel. Bring a large pot of salted water to a boil. Add the haricots verts and cook until just tender, 2 to 4 minutes. Use tongs to transfer to the kitchen towel, then pat dry and transfer to a large bowl. Toss the warm beans with about a quarter of the prepared vinaigrette. Season with flaky sea salt.

Add the potatoes to the boiling water. Cook until fork tender, 10 to 15 minutes. Drain through a fine-mesh sieve, then transfer the warm potatoes to another bowl and toss with about half of the remaining vinaigrette. Season with flaky sea salt.

Arrange the mesclun on a large platter. Drizzle with the remainder of the prepared vinaigrette. Halve the eggs lengthwise and season the cut side of the eggs lightly with flaky sea salt. Arrange the eggs, tomatoes, haricots verts, potatoes, cucumber, radishes, spring onions, tuna, anchovies, and olives in separate piles on top of the mesclun and serve.

note to prepare the eggs | **To hard boil eggs:** Prepare an ice bath in a large bowl and set aside. Bring a large saucepan of salted water to a boil over medium-high heat. Using a slotted spoon, gently add the eggs into the water one at a time. Cook for 12 minutes, adjusting the heat as necessary to maintain a gentle boil. Using a slotted spoon, transfer the eggs to the prepared ice bath and chill for 5 minutes. Peel the eggs and set aside. **To soft boil eggs:** Prepare exactly the same way but cook the eggs for 7 minutes.

The (Chickpea) Picnic Salad

2 shallots, thinly sliced

1 small garlic clove, grated on a Microplane

¼ cup [60 ml] sherry or red wine vinegar

¼ cup [60 ml] fresh lemon juice

Hot sauce, if desired

Fine sea salt

2 tablespoons Dijon mustard

1 teaspoon honey, preferably lavender

½ cup [120 ml] extra-virgin olive oil

¼ cup [30 g] salted capers, soaked, rinsed, and drained

2 tablespoons finely chopped Preserved (Meyer) Lemons (page 81)

8 ounces [230 g] mixed green olives, such as Cerignola, Castelvetrano, and Picholine, pitted

Two 15-ounce [430 g] cans chickpeas, drained, or 1 cup [180 g] dried chickpeas, soaked overnight, cooked, and drained (see Note)

8 to 10 radishes, thinly sliced

2 small seedless cucumbers, thinly sliced

Freshly ground black pepper

The south of France is home to a great many prime picnic spots, but my favorites lie on the jagged shoreline running from the edge of Marseille to Cassis. Some of les Calanques—craggy, narrow, picturesque coves framed by massive limestone cliffs—are more accessible than others, but all are worth the commitment. Once you choose your spot, find people diving off rocks, sunning on the tiny beaches, swimming in the clear, salty Mediterranean. Everyone picnics in one way or another. My way is packing this chickpea salad tossed with a punchy caper-preserved lemon vinaigrette, a bag of chips, plenty of water, maybe a bottle of Citron Pressé, My Way (page 31) or local rosé. The salad travels well, just like you.

Serves 6

In a large bowl, combine the shallots, garlic, vinegar, lemon juice, and hot sauce (if using). Season lightly with salt and set aside for at least 15 minutes (and up to 1 hour).

Whisk in the mustard and honey. Whisking constantly, add the olive oil in a steady stream until emulsified. Stir in the capers and preserved lemon, then add the olives, chickpeas, radishes, and cucumbers. Season to taste with salt and pepper. The salad will keep, stored in an airtight container in the refrigerator, for up to 3 days. CONTINUED

note to make chickpeas | In a large bowl, add about **1 cup [180 g] of dried chickpeas** and enough **water** to cover the chickpeas by 3 inches [7.5 cm]. Soak overnight at room temperature. The next day, drain the chickpeas. Set a large pot over medium heat and add **2 tablespoons of olive oil**. When the oil is hot, halve a **yellow onion** crosswise and cook, cut sides down, until golden brown, 2 to 3 minutes.

Add the drained chickpeas, **one 3-inch [7.5 cm] Parmigiano-Reggiano rind, 1 bay leaf,** and **6 to 8 parsley sprigs**. Pour in enough **fresh water** to cover the beans by 2 inches [5 cm] and bring to a boil over medium-high heat. Season with **fine sea salt**, then lower the heat to a simmer and cook, skimming any scum that rises to the top, until the chickpeas are tender but still hold their shape, anywhere from 30 minutes to 2 hours. Season with **salt and pepper** and cook for another 10 minutes. Remove from the heat and let the chickpeas cool in their broth. Discard the Parmesan rind, onion, bay leaves, and parsley. You can store the chickpeas in their cooking liquid in a covered container in the refrigerator for up to one week. Makes about 3 cups [480 g] cooked and drained chickpeas. (Don't toss the bean cooking liquid when you drain the chickpeas—it's very good. Save it and use as a base for soup.)

Radicchio Salad with Poached Quince

In Provence, you'll most often find quince in the form of pâte de coing—firm, sticky-sweet quince paste. When good, it is undeniably special as an addition to a cheese plate (page 263) or an afternoon snack. While you can make it yourself at home, I prefer to allow others to do that particular work. Instead, when I come across the fuzzy, yellow, wonky-shaped fruits that are hard and astringent and basically impossible when raw, I poach them. It's a simple way to transform their deceptively fragrant yet inedible allure into something that works beautifully with cheese but also in your salads, next to roast meats, on top of yogurt or ice cream, and on and on.

Serves 6

To make the vinaigrette: In a resealable jar, add the shallots and vinegar. Season with fine sea salt and pepper, stir to combine, and let sit for at least 15 minutes. Add the mustard and poaching liquid, then pour in the oil, cover the jar tightly with a lid, and shake to emulsify. Season with fine sea salt and pepper. The vinaigrette will keep, stored in an airtight container in the refrigerator, for up to 3 days.

   To make the salad: Layer the radicchio leaves and poached quince in a serving bowl. Drizzle the vinaigrette over the salad and finish with the walnuts. Season with flaky sea salt and pepper. CONTINUED

VINAIGRETTE

2 shallots, thinly sliced

¼ cup [60 ml] sherry vinegar

Fine sea salt

Freshly ground black pepper

2 tablespoons Dijon mustard

2 teaspoons quince poaching liquid (recipe follows) or honey

½ cup [120 ml] extra-virgin olive oil

SALAD

1 large head Castelfranco or pink radicchio, trimmed and leaves separated, larger leaves roughly torn

2 small or 1 large head red radicchio, trimmed and leaves separated, larger leaves roughly torn

6 poached quince quarters, cored and thinly sliced (recipe follows)

1 cup [120 g] walnuts, toasted

Flaky sea salt

Freshly ground black pepper

Poached Quince

Makes 2 pounds [910 g]

In a medium saucepan, combine 4 cups [960 ml] of water with the sugar. Place the pan over medium heat and bring just to a simmer. Turn the heat to low and cook, stirring gently, just until the sugar dissolves. Turn off the heat and peel and quarter each quince one by one, reserving the peels and cutting out and discarding any brown spots on the flesh. Once each quince is peeled and quartered, immediately add it to the sugar syrup before starting on the next. Gather the reserved peels into a cheesecloth, tie the ends together to seal it into a package, and add to the pan.

Cut a piece of parchment paper into a circle that just fits inside the saucepan.

Turn on the heat again to medium and return the mixture to a simmer. Set the parchment circle on top (it should be touching the surface) and adjust the heat to maintain a very gentle simmer. Cook until the quince pieces are tender and rose pink in color, 1½ to 2 hours. Remove the pan from the heat and set aside to cool completely.

Store the quince in their poaching liquid in the refrigerator for up to 10 days.

note | Quarter your quince before poaching but wait to core them until after they've cooked and you're about to slice and serve. Before cooking, coring quince is unnerving at best; the fruit is very hard and unyielding, the knife dangerously unwieldy in your hand. After the quince is rendered soft and luscious through gentle cooking, it is much easier.

note | You don't *need* need to save the quince peels and add them to the syrup, but they provide a deeper layer of flavor and aroma to the final product, so why would you not?

note | Add aromatics if you like to the poaching syrup at the start: a vanilla bean, a cinnamon stick, star anise, cloves, black peppercorns, a bay leaf. Added aromatics or not, this poaching syrup can and should be used in drinks—alcoholic or otherwise.

1 cup [200 g] granulated sugar

2 pounds [910 g] quince (about 4 to 5 medium)

Celery + Fennel Salad

I make a version of this crunchy, citrusy, caramelized date–topped salad about once a week. Sometimes, depending on my mood and/or what I find at the market, I make it with only fennel or with only celery (in a direct nod to the raw celery salads eaten in Provence on Christmas Eve). Sometimes it's a crumble of cheese or a drizzle of walnut oil and a handful of toasted nuts. I rarely if ever skip the caramelized dates though. A quick toss in a hot pan and some flaky salt is all it takes to turn the sweet dried fruits toward savory. Sometimes, there's no salad at all.

Serves 6

In a large bowl, combine the thinly sliced fennel, celery, and lemon zest and juice. Season with fine sea salt and toss to coat. Let sit for 20 to 30 minutes, tossing occasionally.

Holding the fennel and celery out of the way with clean hands or a spoon, whisk the mustard and hot sauce (if using) into the lemon juice. Toss to coat, then drizzle with ⅓ cup [80 ml] of the olive oil and season with fine sea salt and pepper. Toss the fennel-celery mixture well to coat with the dressing and taste for seasoning. Set aside.

In a medium saucepan set over medium-high heat, add the remaining 1 tablespoon of olive oil. Once the oil is hot, add the dates in a single layer. Cook on the first side until lightly blistered, 45 seconds to 1 minute, then carefully flip the dates and cook for another 30 seconds on the other side. Transfer the dates to a cutting board and sprinkle with flaky sea salt. Coarsely chop and layer on top of the fennel-celery salad, then serve.

3 large fennel bulbs, trimmed, cored and very thinly sliced

8 celery stalks, trimmed and very thinly sliced on the bias

2 lemons, zested and juiced

Fine sea salt

2 tablespoons grainy mustard

Hot sauce, if desired

⅓ cup plus 1 tablespoon [95 ml] extra-virgin olive oil, plus more for serving

Freshly ground black pepper

8 to 10 dates, pitted

Flaky sea salt

Frisée with Roasted Garlic Vinaigrette

Whether I "need" them or not, I can never resist the braids of garlic sold at marchés across the south, the heads prettily threaded together with a little space at the top to tie them wherever you tend to tie them in your kitchen. While Provençal cooking requires plenty of garlic, if I have a surplus to use up and make space for another braid, I'll roast a few heads while the oven is on for something else and use one to make this vinaigrette and the rest in soup, on toast, or stirred into pasta. The garlic metamorphoses into soft, golden, sweetened nuggets to squeeze out and smash together with anchovies, lemon, and vinegar. The thick, potent dressing here both slicks and sticks especially nicely to a jumble of finely curled bitter greens.

Serves 6 | Makes a scant ⅔ cup [160 ml] vinaigrette

Preheat the oven to 400°F [200°C].

To make the vinaigrette: Cut off the top ¼ inch [6 mm] of the garlic head, keeping the head intact. Place the garlic on a piece of aluminum foil, drizzle with 1 tablespoon of the olive oil, and season with salt and pepper. Wrap in the foil and roast until the garlic is very soft and golden, 50 minutes to 1 hour. Set aside to cool completely.

Squeeze the roasted garlic cloves onto a clean cutting board and use the side of a knife to smash them into a smooth paste. Place in a resealable jar along with the anchovies, lemon zest and juice, vinegar, mustard, and honey. Pour in the remaining ⅓ cup [95 ml] of oil, cover the jar tightly with a lid, and shake to emulsify. Taste and season with salt and pepper. The dressing will keep, stored in an airtight container in the refrigerator, for 3 to 4 days.

To make the salad: Transfer the dressing to a large salad bowl. Add the frisée and toss to coat. Serve immediately.

note | I highly recommend adding a tablespoon or so of finely chopped Preserved (Meyer) Lemons (page 81) to this dressing. Be sure to taste before seasoning with salt at the end.

1 head garlic

⅓ cup plus 1 tablespoon [95 ml] extra-virgin olive oil

Fine sea salt

Freshly ground black pepper

4 anchovy fillets, finely chopped

1 small lemon, zested and juiced

1 tablespoon white wine vinegar

1 tablespoon Dijon mustard

1 teaspoon honey, preferably lavender

1 large head frisée, trimmed and torn into 2-inch [5 cm] pieces

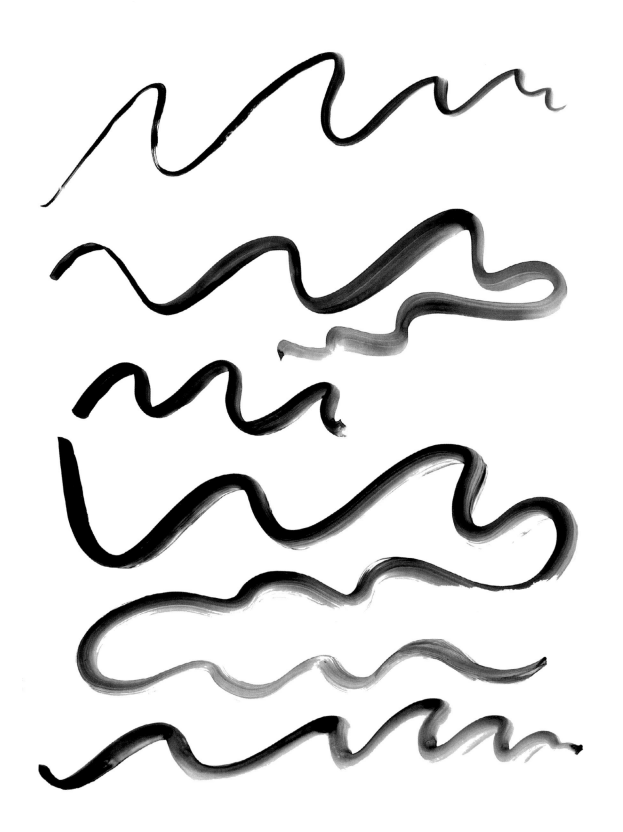

to FINISH

TO FINISH

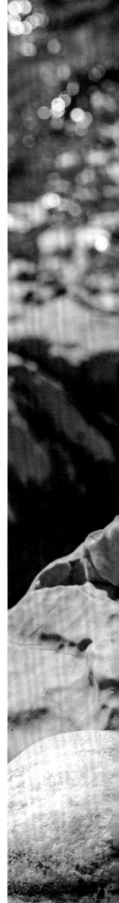

SOMETHING SWEET

Bendita entre los Melones

Both my wife and ex-girlfriend were present when we shot this in Marseille. My other ex-girlfriend edited this very headnote. And that, my friends, is lesbian culture.

Serves 2

Cut the melon in half crosswise. Scoop out and discard the seeds. Add 1 ounce of wine to each half, sprinkle the edges with salt, and serve.

note | While the traditional version features a few ounces of chilled Muscat de Beaumes-de-Venise (a sweet wine from a bit farther north in the region) poured into the chilled melon's center, a modern bar might opt for equal parts dry rosé and cognac or a splash of Vin d'Orange (page 36).

note on the Charentais melon | The small, sweet, green-striped local Charentais melon is considered to be the best in the world. While I have consistently missed the yearly Fête des Melons in Cavaillon by a few days—during which one hundred white Camargue horses run through the center square, okay!!—I make up for it with my own personal fête of melons: heavy, sun-soaked slices sprinkled with salt, slippery cubes wrapped in ham and—a personal favorite—chilled until the refrigerator is perfumed with their scent, then halved and anointed with booze.

note on Bendita entre los Melones | Literally "blessed between the melons," this recipe title is inspired by a Spanish saying, "bendito entre las mujeres" or "blessed among the women."

1 ripe Charentais melon (or other orange-fleshed variety), chilled

2 ounces [60 ml] sweet white wine such as Muscat de Beaume-de-Venise or Sauternes, chilled

Flaky sea salt

Strawberry Gâteau

In France, we enjoy a rolling strawberry season from early spring until the first frosts of autumn. The long, sweet, delicate Gariguette begins. Next comes the juicy, aromatic Ciflorette, the bright red Clery, the heart-shaped Charlotte. Then the ascendance of the tiny in size, big in sweet, acidic flavored Fraise du Bois. The Mara des Bois is the latest to appear.

The beauty of recipe testing and testing and testing for a book means you test throughout multiple seasons, meaning I've made this with multiple varieties. Some hold their shape better, others are sweeter, some are larger, all are highly recommended. And if your strawberry season is more of the "the good stuff peaks in June" variety, use those June berries.

STRAWBERRIES

1 pound [455 g] fresh strawberries, stemmed and halved

1 tablespoon granulated sugar

Pinch of flaky sea salt

⅓ cup [80 ml] dry rosé

GÂTEAU

1 tablespoon unsalted European butter

½ cup plus 2 tablespoons [130 g] granulated sugar

1¾ cups [245 g] all-purpose flour

¾ teaspoon baking powder

½ teaspoon flaky sea salt, plus more to finish

¼ teaspoon baking soda

2 large eggs

½ cup [120 ml] extra-virgin olive oil

⅓ cup [80 ml] strawberry-rosé soaking liquid

1½ teaspoons vanilla extract or ½ vanilla bean, split and scraped, pod reserved for another use

Crème fraîche, for serving

Makes one 9-inch [23 cm] gâteau

To make the strawberries: In a medium bowl, combine the strawberries, sugar, and salt. Add the rosé, toss gently to combine, and set aside to macerate for 1 hour, stirring occasionally.

To make the gâteau: Preheat the oven to 325°F [165°C]. Butter a 9-inch [23 cm] round springform pan. Sprinkle the pan evenly with 1 tablespoon of the granulated sugar.

In a medium bowl, whisk together the flour, baking powder, salt, and baking soda.

In a separate medium bowl, vigorously whisk together ½ cup [100 g] of the sugar and the eggs until lightened in color and the sugar dissolves, about 2 minutes. Whisk in the olive oil, strawberry-rosé soaking liquid (reserve any remaining liquid for later), and the vanilla. CONTINUED

Use a spatula to gently fold in the flour mixture until just combined. Transfer to the prepared pan and sprinkle with the remaining 1 tablespoon of sugar. Arrange the berries on top in a circle, cut-side up (or just dump them all on evenly). Bake until the gâteau is golden and set and a toothpick inserted in the center comes out clean, 1 hour to 75 minutes, gently rotating the pan halfway through baking.

Brush the top of the gâteau with the remaining strawberry-rosé soaking liquid, sprinkle with salt, and let cool in the pan for 15 to 20 minutes before removing. Cool completely on a cooling rack or serve warm with crème fraîche. Leftover slices of the gâteau will keep, covered, in the refrigerator, for 3 to 4 days.

note | Sure, yes, the recipe title here is *Strawberry Gâteau* but depending on what you have/love it could just as easily be *abricot gâteau* or *donut peach gâteau* or *currant gâteau* or *cherry gâteau* . . . you get the idea.

Tarte au Citron

Local legend says that when Eve and Adam were exiled from the Garden of Eden, Eve took a lemon with her, eventually burying it in the spot that would become Menton. The seaside town sits between the Alpes Maritimes and the Mediterranean and its valley benefits from a microclimate that is uniquely protected in winter, rising a few degrees warmer than the rest of the Côte d'Azur, and cooled in summer. In short, the ideal spot for citrus. While Menton is now home to over one hundred different varieties of fruit, the Citron de Menton is still legend—oval, bright yellow, intensely fragrant, a peel rich in essential oils and a slightly acidic but not bitter taste. Find yourself in the south of France with easy access to Menton lemons? Use them in this tart. Otherwise, a mix of Meyer and standard very much works.

CRUST

12 tablespoons [165 g] unsalted European butter, chilled and cut into cubes, plus more for the pan

1½ cups [210 g] all-purpose flour

½ cup [60 g] confectioners' sugar, plus more for serving

2 teaspoons finely chopped Preserved (Meyer) Lemon rind [page 81] (see Note)

¼ teaspoon fine sea salt

FILLING

3 large eggs

3 large egg yolks

3 medium organic Meyer (or Menton!) lemons, zested and juiced

1 to 3 standard lemons, juiced (whatever is needed to get 1 cup [240 ml] juice total)

¾ cup [150 g] granulated sugar

¼ teaspoon fine sea salt

12 tablespoons [165 g] cold unsalted European butter

Confectioners' sugar, for dusting

Flaky sea salt

Makes one 9-inch [23 cm] tarte

To make the crust: Butter a 9-inch [23 cm] tart pan.

In the bowl of a food processor, combine the flour, confectioners' sugar, preserved lemon rind, and fine sea salt. Pulse to combine, then scatter the butter cubes on top and pulse until a crumbly dough forms. It is ready when it holds together when you pinch it with your fingers.

Transfer the dough to the prepared tart pan and use your hands to press it evenly into the bottom and up the sides of the pan; the layer should be about ¼ inch [6 mm] thick. Place the pan in the freezer until the dough is very firm, 30 to 40 minutes, or in the refrigerator up to overnight.

Preheat the oven to 350°F [180°C].

Place the tart pan on a baking sheet lined with parchment paper. Use a fork to prick the bottom of the dough all over. Place the pan on the prepared baking sheet and line with parchment paper so it covers the crust's bottom and sides, then add dried beans or pie weights on top of the paper. Bake for 20 minutes, then remove the paper and weights. CONTINUED

Continue baking until the crust is lightly golden brown, 5 to 8 minutes more. While the crust finishes baking, make the filling.

To make the filling: Set a fine-mesh sieve over a bowl. In a large saucepan, combine the eggs, egg yolks, Meyer lemon juice and zest, standard lemon juice, sugar, and fine sea salt. Whisk together, then set over medium heat and add the butter. Cook, stirring constantly with a wooden spoon or silicone spatula, until the mixture noticeably thickens and starts to bubble, 6 to 8 minutes.

Strain through the sieve then immediately pour the curd into the pre-baked crust (the crust can still be warm) and use the back of the spoon or a spatula to spread the curd evenly into the shell. Bake until the curd is set and the center of the filling is only slightly jiggly, 10 to 15 minutes. Be sure to check the tarte and cover the edges with aluminum foil if they are getting too brown.

Cool completely, then refrigerate and serve chilled. Tarte au citron can be eaten the same day it's made but tbh it is even better when refrigerated overnight and served chilled the next day. Do that if you can, then dust with confectioners' sugar and sprinkle with flaky sea salt just before serving. Leftover tarte au citron will keep, covered, in the refrigerator for up to 3 days.

note | If you don't have preserved lemons on hand, make the crust with the zest of 1 lemon, grated on a Microplane, and increase the fine sea salt in the crust to ½ teaspoon.

La Tropézienne
EVERYONE LOVES THIS TARTE

CAKE

½ cup [120 ml] whole milk, warm

2¼ teaspoons active dry yeast

2 cups [280 g] all-purpose flour

¼ cup [50 g] granulated sugar

2 large eggs plus 1 egg yolk, at room temperature

1½ teaspoons pure vanilla extract

1½ teaspoons orange blossom water

1 teaspoon fine sea salt

6 tablespoons [85 g] unsalted European butter, cubed and at room temperature, plus more for the pan

1 egg white, beaten

3 tablespoons pearl sugar

PASTRY CREAM

1½ cups [480 ml] whole milk

½ vanilla bean, split lengthwise, seeds scraped (or 2 teaspoons pure vanilla extract)

Pinch of fine sea salt

½ cup [100 g] granulated sugar

¼ cup [35 g] cornstarch

5 large egg yolks

2 tablespoons cold unsalted European butter, cubed

ASSEMBLY

¼ cup [60 ml] heavy cream, very cold

The lives of Brigitte Bardot and I don't have a lot of overlapping storylines but we both really, really enjoyed our first taste of Tarte Tropézienne. On her end, the story goes that a Polish baker, Alexandre Micka, served Mlle Bardot a slice while she was filming in Saint-Tropez. She loved it so much she named it La Tarte Tropézienne. On mine, I spent a tropézienne-hopping, yacht-dodging week in the town, which looks and feels quite a bit different than the small, charming fishing village my friend in cake Brigitte arrived at in 1955.

While the original tarte's exact recipe remains a tightly held secret, the concept is clear: a bready, egg-rich brioche topped with crunchy pearl sugar and layered with a smooth, sweet, creamy filling. I've seen tropéziennes filled with Nutella, flavored with rum, and studded with strawberries, but this recipe adheres as closely as I could get to the original. While it does take some time and a few different components, you can make each in advance (I've noted these in the recipe) and assemble the tropézienne the day you plan to eat it.

Makes one 9-inch [23 cm] tropézienne

To make the cake: In the bowl of a stand mixer fitted with a paddle attachment, combine the warm milk and yeast. Set aside for 5 minutes to dissolve the yeast. Add the flour and sugar to the bowl and mix to combine. With the mixer running on low speed, add the eggs and egg yolk one at a time, waiting until each is incorporated before adding the next. Add the vanilla, orange blossom water, and salt, then increase the speed to medium and beat for 2 minutes. The batter will be smooth and thick.

Increase the speed to medium-high and add the butter cubes a few at a time, pressing each between your fingertips to temper before adding and waiting until the cubes are incorporated before adding the next. CONTINUED

Continue to mix until the batter is very smooth, stretchy, and lightened in color, about 5 minutes more. The batter will be quite thick but less thick than a standard bread dough. Use a spatula to scrape down and clean the sides of the bowl, gathering the batter into a round shape, then cover the bowl tightly with plastic wrap or reusable beeswax wrap; set aside in a warm, draft-free place until it just about doubles in size, 60 to 75 minutes.

Lightly butter a 9-inch [23 cm] springform pan. Use a spatula to transfer the batter from the bowl, gently spreading it evenly in the pan. Cover the pan tightly with plastic wrap or reusable beeswax wrap and set aside to rise again in a warm, draft-free place for 30 minutes.

Preheat the oven to 350°F [180°C].

Use a pastry brush to lightly and gently brush the top of the cake with the egg white. Sprinkle evenly with the pearl sugar. Bake until the cake is golden brown and cooked through, 20 to 25 minutes; a skewer inserted into the center of the brioche should come out clean. Transfer to a cooling rack and set aside to cool for 20 minutes. Carefully remove the sides of the springform pan and let the cake cool completely. (The baked cake will keep for 1 day, wrapped tightly in plastic wrap and stored at room temperature.)

To make the pastry cream: In a small saucepan, combine the milk, vanilla bean seeds and pod (if using), and salt. Bring to just a boil, then remove from the heat and set aside to steep for 20 to 30 minutes.

In a medium bowl, whisk together the sugar, cornstarch, and egg yolks. Whisking constantly, slowly add about a quarter of the warm milk mixture to the eggs. Add another quarter of the milk, whisking to combine, then the rest of the milk. Return the mixture to the saucepan, place over medium heat, and cook, whisking constantly, until the pastry cream starts to thicken, 4 to 5 minutes. Once it thickens, pause whisking for a few seconds to check for bubbles. Once the custard begins to bubble, continue whisking for 1 minute more.

Transfer the hot pastry cream to a clean bowl and, if using vanilla extract instead of the bean, whisk it in. Set aside to cool for a few minutes, then whisk in the cold butter, one or two pieces at a time, until all the butter is incorporated and the pastry cream is smooth. Immediately cover the surface with plastic wrap so it is directly touching the cream and let cool completely in the refrigerator, at least 2 to 3 hours. (You can make the pastry cream up to 3 days in advance and store, covered, in the refrigerator.)

To finish: When you're ready to assemble the tropézienne, use a serrated knife to slice the cake in half horizontally. Place the bottom layer of the cake on a serving platter, reserving the top half.

In a large bowl, add the heavy cream and whisk until firm peaks form. Remove the pastry cream from the refrigerator. Remove the vanilla bean pod from the pastry cream (if necessary) and whisk to loosen it and smooth any lumps. Add about half of the whipped cream to the pastry cream and use a spatula to stir it together. Add the remaining whipped cream and gently fold together until just combined. Spread the filling over the bottom cake layer, leaving a ¼-inch [6 mm] border. Place the top layer of cake on top, pressing it gently. Chill in the refrigerator for at least 30 minutes or up to 8 hours (covered lightly in plastic wrap or reusable beeswax wrap) before serving. Leftover slices of the tropézienne will keep, covered in the refrigerator, for 3 to 4 days.

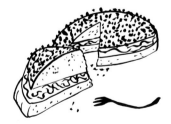

note | Definitely use a stand mixer for this recipe. A hand-held or hands-only approach won't have the strength needed to give the brioche the lift it needs.

note | The pearl sugar sprinkled on top is an important part of the recipe. You can find it online or in specialty stores. If you really must have tropézienne now, crush sugar cubes into chunky pieces.

Tarte à la Raspberry

As soon as you arrive in summertime Provence, the unmistakable high-volume chirping hum of cigales (cicadas) greets you. The unrelenting serenade becomes louder the hotter it gets, slowing only when the sun sets and the air cools. It's a surround-sound sensory experience, one I've begun to crave each year as summer sets in. The volume is both loud and soothing, a combination that sends me either to the kitchen or for a nap. When it's the former, I make this.

Makes one 9-inch [23 cm] tart

CRUST

½ cup plus 1 tablespoon [126 g] unsalted European butter, chilled and cubed, plus more for the pan

½ cup [60 g] confectioners' sugar

1 teaspoon flaky sea salt

2 large eggs

2 cups [280 g] all-purpose flour, plus more for dusting

SMASHED RASPBERRY FILLING

1½ cups [170 g] ripe raspberries, gently washed and dried

1 teaspoon honey, preferably lavender

Flaky sea salt

CRÈME FRAÎCHE FILLING

¾ cup [180 ml] heavy whipping cream

1 to 2 tablespoons confectioners' sugar

¼ teaspoon flaky sea salt

½ cup [120 g] crème fraîche

ASSEMBLY

3 cups [340 g] ripe raspberries, gently washed and dried

Flaky sea salt

To make the crust: In a stand mixer fitted with a paddle attachment, combine the butter, confectioners' sugar, and salt; beat until light and fluffy. Scrape down the sides of the bowl, then add one of the eggs (reserve the second egg for the egg wash) and beat until incorporated. Stir in the flour just until a dough forms and holds together. Gather it into a ball and wrap in plastic or reusable beeswax wrap. Refrigerate for at least 1 hour and up to 3 days.

Lightly butter a 9-inch [23 cm] tart pan with a removable bottom. On a lightly floured surface or between layers of parchment paper, roll out the dough into an 11-inch [28 cm] circle. Transfer to the tart pan and gently press the dough into the base and sides of the pan. Trim the edges and refrigerate for 1 hour.

Preheat the oven to 400°F [200°C].

Use a fork to prick the bottom of the dough all over. Place the pan on a baking sheet and line with parchment paper so it covers the crust's bottom and sides, then add dried beans or pie weights on top of the paper. Bake for 20 minutes, then remove the paper and weights. Beat the second egg with a fork, then use a pastry brush to brush it evenly over the crust's bottom and sides. Continue to bake until the crust is nicely golden brown, 10 to 15 minutes more. Set aside to cool completely. CONTINUED

To make the smashed raspberry filling: In a small
bowl, add the raspberries, honey, and a small pinch of salt.
Use the back of a spoon or fork to smash until a rough
purée forms and everything is well mixed.

To make the crème fraîche filling: Place a large metal
bowl and whisk in the freezer to chill for 10 minutes. In the
chilled bowl, add the heavy cream, confectioners' sugar, and
salt and whisk vigorously until medium peaks form, 3 to
5 minutes. Gently whisk in the crème fraîche.

To assemble: Use an offset spatula to spread the
smashed raspberry filling in a thin layer across the bottom
of the cooled crust. Gently spoon the prepared crème
fraîche filling over the top. Clean the offset spatula and
use it to smooth the crème fraîche filling into an even
layer. Arrange the raspberries in a single layer over the tart,
sprinkle with salt, and serve immediately or store in the
refrigerator until ready to serve. The tart can be assembled
up to 3 hours ahead of time and leftover slices will keep,
covered, in the refrigerator, for up to 3 days.

Reine Claude (or Other, Lesser Plums) Clafoutis

Small, green, and sweet, the Reine Claude is plum royalty. Also called greengage plums, they arrive in Provençal markets in August and last through September stacked in triumphant, tumbling towers to be eaten fresh out of hand, cooked into jams and tarts, and preserved in eau de vie for colder, less reine-rich days. To know them is to love them, but I love them most blanketed in custard and baked into clafoutis. Serve for dessert, saving any leftovers for the next morning. An overnight in the refrigerator concentrates the clafoutis further, the densely rich, creamy, plum-dotted spoonfuls best savored barefoot and solo directly out of the cold dish, hot coffee at hand. It's breakfast, for queens.

Makes one 10-inch [25 cm] clafoutis

Preheat the oven to 375°F [190°C].

In a small saucepan over medium heat, melt the butter and cook, swirling occasionally, until it smells nutty and toasted and the milk solids turn golden brown, 3 to 4 minutes. Remove from the heat immediately and cool completely.

Brush the bottom of a 10-inch [25 cm] round baking pan or dish with butter. Add the plums in an even layer to the baking pan.

In a blender, combine the cooled browned butter, milk, heavy cream, eggs, flour, ¼ cup [50 g] of the sugar, and the salt. Blend for 1 minute. Gently pour the mixture over the plums and sprinkle with the remaining 1 tablespoon of sugar. Bake until the top is lightly browned and the custard is just set, 35 to 40 minutes. Serve warm or at room temperature. Leftover clafoutis will keep, covered, in the refrigerator for up to 3 days.

2 tablespoons unsalted European butter, plus more for the pan

1½ pounds [680 g] Reine Claude plums (or other plums such as Mirabelle or Damson), halved and pitted

¾ cup [180 ml] whole milk

½ cup [120 ml] heavy cream

3 large eggs

½ cup [70 g] all-purpose flour

¼ cup plus 1 tablespoon [65 g] granulated sugar

¼ teaspoon flaky sea salt

Figs + Crème

The first ever trip I took to Provence-Alpes-Côte d'Azur, I rented a house with a fig tree. To this day, there's nothing that brings me back to the region faster nor anything I love more to eat than a fresh fig—ripe and sunwarm and sapphic. When I'm not in close proximity to a tree weighted with figs, I channel the Provençal sun and make these.

Serves 6

Preheat the oven to 400°F [200°C].

Arrange the halved figs cut-side up in a single layer in a large baking dish with the rosemary, if using, and bay leaf. Drizzle the figs with honey (warm the honey slightly if needed to allow it to drizzle freely). Dot with the butter, add the vermouth, and season with salt.

Cover the dish tightly with aluminum foil and bake for 30 minutes. Uncover the dish and continue baking for about 10 minutes more, until the figs are very tender and soft and the juices are syrupy. Juice the lime to taste over the top. The figs will keep, refrigerated and stored with their syrup, for up to 4 days and can be served warm or cold.

When you are ready to serve, place a large metal bowl and whisk in the freezer to chill for 10 minutes. In the chilled bowl, add the heavy cream and a pinch of salt. Whisk until medium peaks form. Transfer to a bowl and serve with figs and a sprinkle of salt.

1½ pounds [680 g] fresh, ripe figs, stems removed and figs halved lengthwise

2 sprigs fresh rosemary (optional)

1 bay leaf

1 tablespoon honey, preferably lavender

1 tablespoon unsalted European butter, cut into small pieces

3 tablespoons blanc vermouth (see Note)

Flaky sea salt

1 lime

1 cup [240 ml] heavy cream

note | If you would like to make this without alcohol, use water instead. If you don't have blanc vermouth in the house and still want to use alcohol, use sweet vermouth, Lillet Blanc, or Vin d'Orange (page 36) or a dry red, rosé, or white wine.

note | Sometimes, instead of whipped cream, I'll serve these figs with a bowl of crème fraîche or crème crue (made with unpasteurized milk).

Holiday Cookies, Provence Edition

The purity of a holiday cookie box! Or tin! The promise, the possibilities! When in Provence, I include **Navettes**, boat-shaped biscuit cookies made with fleur d'oranger and olive oil and traditionally eaten in Marseille to celebrate Candlemas in February. Also, little squares of hazelnut-studded **Nougat**, a soft, white, honeyed part of Provence's treize desserts de Noël (the traditional thirteen desserts served on Christmas Eve). And because they come with me wherever the holiday season ends up, one cookie that isn't Provençal at all, **My Mom's**.

Navettes

¼ cup [55 g] unsalted European butter, at room temperature

¾ cup plus 2 tablespoons [180 g] granulated sugar

3 large eggs, at room temperature

2 tablespoons extra-virgin olive oil

3 teaspoons orange blossom water

2¾ cups [385 g] all-purpose flour

¼ teaspoon fine sea salt

Makes sixteen 4-inch [10 cm] navettes

In a stand mixer fitted with a paddle attachment, combine the butter and ¾ cup [150 g] of the granulated sugar; beat until light and fluffy. Add two of the eggs, the olive oil, and 2 teaspoons of the orange blossom water and beat until the eggs are incorporated. Stir in the flour and salt just until combined.

Divide the dough in half, form each half into a 4-inch [10 cm] round, and wrap each round in plastic or reusable beeswax wrap. Refrigerate for at least 1 hour and up to 3 days. (The dough can also be frozen for up to 3 months.)

Preheat the oven to 350°F [180°C]. Line a baking sheet with parchment paper.

In a small bowl, whisk together the remaining egg and the remaining 1 teaspoon orange blossom water until frothy; set aside. Line two baking sheets with parchment paper.

CONTINUED

Cut each chilled dough round into 8 equal pieces and, working one piece at a time on an unfloured work surface, use your hands to roll each piece into a 3½-inch [9 cm] log, about ½ inch [12 mm] thick. Flatten the logs slightly, then use your fingers to pinch together each end to form a 4-inch [10 cm] boat-shaped cookie. Use a paring knife to carefully cut a 2½-inch [6 cm] long slit in the center of the boat, cutting just halfway down through the dough. Use your fingers to gently push the slit open slightly; they should resemble small boats. Transfer the navettes to the prepared baking sheets.

Brush the tops of the navettes with the orange blossom egg wash and sprinkle with the remaining 2 tablespoons of sugar. Bake until the navettes are set and lightly golden around the edges, 18 to 20 minutes. Let cool for 5 minutes on the baking sheet, then transfer to a cooling rack and cool completely before serving. Navettes will last, stored in an airtight container, for up to 5 days (you can also freeze them in an airtight container for up to 3 months).

Hazelnut Nougat

Makes about fifty 1-inch [2.5 cm] squares

Line an 8-inch [20 cm] square baking pan with one sheet of parchment paper lengthwise, then add a second sheet crosswise, letting the edges hang over the sides of the pan. Spray the paper with nonstick spray. If using edible confectioners' rice paper, trim the sheets into two 8-inch [20 cm] squares and place one trimmed sheet in the prepared pan, shiny-side down.

In a medium pot, set over medium heat, add the honey, 1¼ cups [250 g] of the sugar, and 3 tablespoons of water. Stir gently to combine, then place over medium-high heat. Cook the mixture, swirling the pan occasionally, until it reads 330°F [65°C] on a candy thermometer.

While the honey-sugar syrup is cooking, begin whipping the egg whites. In the bowl of a stand mixer fitted with the whisk attachment, combine the egg whites and the remaining 1 tablespoon of sugar. Beat on medium-high speed until soft peaks form, then lower the speed to medium and, with the mixer running, very slowly and carefully add the hot honey-sugar syrup. Increase the speed to high and whisk until the sides of the bowl start to feel a bit cooler and the nougat texture begins to become rougher, about 15 minutes. Lower the speed to low and add the vanilla and salt, stirring to combine, then, working quickly so the nougat doesn't stiffen up too much, add the warm hazelnuts, stirring to combine.

Immediately transfer the nougat to the prepared baking sheet and evenly spread it into the pan; the nougat should be about ½-inch [12 mm] thick. Set a piece of lightly greased parchment paper or the remaining edible confectioners' rice paper sheets on top of the nougat and press down to smooth (you can also use a lightly greased offset spatula or spoon to smooth it out). If using candied oranges, skip the top layer of paper and gently press them in a single layer directly on top of the nougat. Set aside to cool overnight at room temperature. CONTINUED

Parchment paper

Two 8-by-11–inch [20 by 28 cm] sheets of edible confectioners' rice paper or wafer paper, if desired

¾ cup [255 g] honey, preferably orange blossom or lavender

1¼ cups plus 1 tablespoon [265 g] granulated sugar

2 large egg whites, at room temperature

1 teaspoon vanilla extract

1 teaspoon flaky sea salt

2 cups [240 g] toasted hazelnuts, warm

8 to 10 candied orange wheels, if desired

Lift the nougat out of the pan using the baking paper edges and transfer to a cutting board. Use a sharp knife to cut the nougat into 1-inch [2.5 cm] squares or any desired shape. (For easier cutting, I like to dip my knife in hot water to warm the blade, then I wipe the blade dry. I cut the nougat, occasionally reheating the knife and wiping dry as needed. Otherwise, I'll spray my knife with nonstick spray.) Serve or wrap in parchment paper or candy wrappers. Store in an airtight container for up 3 weeks.

note | Traditionally, nougat of Montélimar is made with at least 30 percent almonds (or 28 percent almonds and 2 percent pistachios). I prefer mine with hazelnuts, but feel free to swap in another nut such as almonds, pistachios, or walnuts, and/or add a handful of dried fruit.

note | Edible confectioners' rice paper or wafer paper can be found in specialty shops and online. As its name indicates, edible confectioners' rice paper or wafer paper is in fact edible and thus doesn't need to be removed. I love using it for nougat as I find it's the least annoying way to deal with nougat's inherent stickiness and the best way to preserve the final shape. If I don't have wafer paper and my nougat is looking a little sticky on top, I'll lightly dust the top of the finished nougat with a 50/50 mix of confectioners' sugar and cornstarch.

note | Nougat is a weather-dependent food, by which I mean humidity and/or extreme heat are not your friends here. If it's hot or humid and you simply must have nougat (lol) know that the nougat will take longer to set up (it definitely won't set up perfectly) and the finished nougat will soften, so keep it stored in an airtight container in the refrigerator and serve chilled.

My Mom's

Makes fifty to sixty 3-inch [7.5 cm] cookies and 2 cups [480 ml] frosting

To make the cookies: In a medium bowl, whisk together the flour, baking soda, cream of tartar, and fine sea salt; set aside.

In a stand mixer fitted with a paddle attachment, combine the butter and confectioners' sugar; beat until light and fluffy. Add the egg and vanilla and beat until incorporated. Stir in the flour mixture just until combined. Divide the dough in half and form each half into a round. Wrap in plastic or reusable beeswax wrap and refrigerate for at least 2 hours and up to 3 days. (The dough can also be frozen for up to 3 months.)

Line a baking sheet with parchment paper. Remove one of the dough rounds from the refrigerator. On a lightly floured piece of parchment paper, roll out the dough into a ⅛-inch [4 mm] thick round. Transfer to the baking sheet, cover with a second piece of parchment paper, and place in the refrigerator for 15 to 20 minutes (this dough is quite buttery, and this chill time will allow you to cut out the shapes with ease). Repeat with the second round of dough.

Preheat the oven to 350°F [180°C].

Cut out shapes from the rolled and chilled dough and transfer to parchment paper–lined baking sheets, spacing the shapes about 1 inch [2.5 cm] apart. Bake until the cookies are set and lightly golden around the edges, 7 to 10 minutes. Let cool slightly on the pan, then transfer to a cooling rack to cool completely.

To make the frosting: In a stand mixer fitted with a whisk attachment, add the butter and beat until it is very soft and slightly lightened. Add the flaky sea salt, then, with the mixer running, gradually add in about half of the confectioners' sugar, whisking until combined, scraping down the sides of the bowl as needed. Add the vanilla and 2 tablespoons of the heavy cream and mix until smooth. Continue adding the remaining confectioners' sugar. Finish with the remaining 1 tablespoon of heavy cream, mixing until very smooth. Frost the cookies, decorating with sprinkles (if using). Place on a cooling rack until the frosting sets, 1 to 2 hours, then store, in an airtight container, for up to 5 days.

COOKIES

2½ cups [350 g] all-purpose flour, plus more for dusting

1 teaspoon baking soda

1 teaspoon cream of tartar

¼ teaspoon fine sea salt

1 cup [220 g] unsalted European butter, at room temperature

1½ cups [180 g] confectioners' sugar

1 large egg

1½ teaspoons pure vanilla extract

FROSTING

½ cup [110 g] unsalted European butter, at room temperature

Pinch flaky sea salt

3 cups [360 g] confectioners' sugar, sifted

1 teaspoon pure vanilla extract

3 tablespoons heavy whipping cream

Sprinkles, dragées, or edible sugar pearls, if desired

Candied Kumquats

During the few weeks I spent in Plascassier one January, the kumquat tree in La Pitchoune's garden was a siren song of tiny, bright orange fruit. I finalized this recipe in its (and Julia's) long shadow, but the candied inspiration comes from farther to the Provençal east. In Apt, the tradition of fruits confits dates to the fourteenth century, and to this day, master confectioners magic whole fruits from fresh to candied by immersing the oranges, plums, pears, figs, clementines, apricots, melons, lemons, et al. in sugar syrup, gradually increasing the ratio of sugar to water until the fruit is thoroughly sweetened, skin to center. The process for larger fruits can take days or weeks or months, and I'm very happy to leave that work to the fine people of Apt. At home, kumquats are small enough to transform into sweet, glasslike versions of themselves in the span of a sunny winter afternoon.

Makes 1 pound [455 g] candied kumquats

Cut a piece of parchment paper into a circle that just fits inside a medium saucepan.

In a medium saucepan, add the kumquats and cover with cold water. Bring to a boil and cook for 1 minute, then drain through a colander, discarding the water. Return the fruit to the pot, cover again with cold water, and bring to a boil for a second time. Again, cook for 1 minute, then drain through a colander. Repeat this process for a third and final time, then set the kumquats aside to cool slightly.

In the same pot, add 1 cup [240 ml] of water and the sugar. Bring to a gentle simmer over medium heat, stirring to dissolve the sugar. Lower the heat to medium-low and let the sugar syrup simmer and slightly reduce for about 10 minutes. While the sugar syrup cooks, use a paring knife to gently pierce each blanched kumquat a few times, then add to the pot with the sugar syrup. Top with the parchment circle and cook for 40 to 50 minutes. The kumquats should look glossy and slightly transparent. CONTINUED

1 pound [455 g] kumquats

2 cups [400 g] granulated sugar

Remove the pan from the heat and let the kumquats cool completely in the sugar syrup at room temperature. Once completely cooled, transfer the kumquats and syrup to an airtight container and store in the refrigerator. The candied kumquats will keep in the refrigerator, completely covered in their syrup, for 1 month.

note | The syrup the kumquats are cooked and stored in is just as special as the fruits of your labor themselves. Use in cocktails, combine it with sparkling water and a squeeze of fresh juice, or drizzle it over yogurt or ice cream.

note | I like the fruits to speak for themselves but I'm also not there to stop you from adding a vanilla bean or cinnamon stick or a few peppercorns or cloves or a bay leaf to the sugar syrup.

Gueule de Bois Currants

These tiny, boozy berries are *that* easy to eat, so when you set them out in lieu of a digestif, be sure to warn guests to exercise caution lest they wake up avec une gueule de bois (with a hangover, in French; literally it means *wooden mouth*).

Makes 1 pound [455 g] currants

In a clean, resealable 1-liter jar, gently layer in about one-third of the currants. Sprinkle with ⅓ cup [65 g] of the sugar, then repeat twice more with the remaining currants and sugar until they are completely added to the jar. Pour the cognac over the top, cover the jar tightly with the lid, and gently turn the jar up and down a few times to disperse and start dissolving the sugar (don't worry if it doesn't all dissolve quite yet).

Keep in a cool place for 1 month, turning the jar up and down gently every few days. After 1 month, transfer to the refrigerator. The currants will keep for 1 year (or more) in the refrigerator.

note | The cognac syrup the currants sit in is a treat itself. It nods toward crème de cassis but is entirely its own thing. That said, feel free to use it in a similar fashion, stirred into a sparkling or still wine. Drop in a strand of currants too while you're at it.

1 pound [455 g] red currants (about 4 cups), rinsed and set aside to dry

1 cup [200 g] granulated sugar

2 cups [480 ml] cognac

VOULEZ-VOUS ENCORE

AFTER-DINNER DRINKING

Absolutely, sure, after-dinner drinking can mean boozy drinks, but it also can mean other beverages. By this time in the night, perhaps the point isn't to get drunk, but rather to aid in digestion, body and spirit.

To that, if what you want is a drink with ABV, look to darker spirits and liqueurs. Your **amaros**, your **cognacs**, your **whiskeys**, your **génépis**. Set the bottles directly on the table and pull out the cute little cups you keep buying and never use (just me?). In Provence, it's not uncommon to both start and end the night with **Vin d'Orange** (page 36), **Muscat de Beaumes-de-Venise**, or a local **wild thyme liqueur** (Farigoule, made in Haute-Provence, is great).

Should you want a mixed drink, might I suggest something easy? It's been a long night; you're done with the work. Equal-parts drinks are your friends here: **half vermouth (sweet) + half also vermouth (dry)** or **half gin + half vermouth (dry)** or **one-third cognac + one-third Lillet Blanc + one-third bitter liqueur (Salers, Suze, génépi)**.

Your no-ABV option is a gimme: **coffee**. Smart ones pre-grind the beans and portion them into a French press before the night even starts. Once digestif hour hits, brew and set out more little cups. If no one takes you up on coffee, drink it iced in the morning.

Want something hot that won't keep you up all night? Provence's **tisane (herbal infusion)** game is on point. Look especially for lemon verbena, mint, chamomile, and tilleul (linden). You can use the herbs/flowers fresh or you can tie them into bunches and hang them upside down in a dry place for about 2 weeks until fully dried. Once dried, pick off the leaves and transfer them to clean, airtight jars to keep for up to 1 year. Whenever you want to drink a tisane, transfer a few tablespoons to a tea strainer or pot with a built-in strainer, pour hot, boiling water over the top, and steep for 3 to 5 minutes. Maybe serve with a spoonful of lavender honey.

BOIRE QUELQUE CHOSE

THE (MODERN) PROVENÇAL CHEESE PLATE

"Entre la poire et le fromage" is a French expression that translates directly to "between the pear and the cheese."

Colloquially it can mean "toward the end of the meal," that magic, convivial moment when everyone around the table is relaxed and (nearly) sated and conversation and laughter flow freely. In French "entre la poire et le fromage" is also used more generally to illustrate a free moment or moment of relaxation between any two events or situations.

You might think the order should be reversed. In modern France, it's common to eat cheese first, followed by a sweet pear or a sweet slice of gâteau. But the idiom dates back to a time when the fruit was eaten first, and the cheese last—hence the placement of The (Modern) Provençal Cheese Plate in this book.

Regardless of when cheese is set on the table—before dessert, after dessert, as dessert—I hope it finds you in a moment of relaxation.

The cheese plate can simply be that: one perfectly ripe cheese, set on the plate. This minimalist presentation is best offered when a larger dessert is waiting in the wings.

If the cheese plate is the event, however, one must follow one's star on the cheese plate. It's simply the only way! In Provence, goat cheese reigns. Sold in various stages of ripeness, from mild and fresh to deeply aged; shaped in triangles, squares, thick and thin rounds, or logs; dusted with herbs or spices or ash or flowers; wrapped in chestnut or grape leaves. Start there, shooting for a variety in shape and texture (and, if you like, milk type). Then add to it.

Maybe it's a smashed ripe persimmon, candied oranges, a handful of very good and nicely toasted nuts, a slick slice of honeycomb, that jar of very good jam you're keeping in the cupboard for a special occasion. Maybe it's something homemade: Pâte de Coings with Hazelnuts (recipe follows), Abricots au Vinaigre (recipe also follows), slices of Poached Quince (page 214), Candied Kumquats (page 255), Gueule de Bois Currants (page 259), Roasted Grapes (yet again, recipe follows!). The point here is that eating very good cheese is not just for your aunt with good taste.

ENTRE LA POIRE ET LE FROMAGE

Pâte de Coings (Quince Paste) with Hazelnuts

¼ cup [30 g] whole hazelnuts, toasted

6 ounces [170 g] quince paste

Finely chop the hazelnuts and place them in a shallow bowl. Cut the quince paste into ½-inch [12 mm] cubes and add to the bowl a few at a time, tossing them gently and pressing slightly to adhere. Use immediately or store in a covered container in the refrigerator for up to 2 weeks.

Abricots au Vinaigre

4 apricots

⅓ cup [80 ml] sherry or red wine vinegar

1 teaspoon honey (preferably lavender)

10 whole black or pink peppercorns

One 3-inch [7.5 cm] piece lemon peel

1 bay leaf

Fine sea salt

Quarter the apricots lengthwise, discarding the pits. Add to a heatproof bowl and set aside. In a medium saucepan over medium heat, add the sherry, honey, peppercorns, lemon peel, bay leaf, and a pinch of salt. Bring to a simmer, stirring to dissolve the honey. Remove from the heat and pour the hot mixture directly over the apricots. Set aside to marinate at room temperature for 2 hours. Use immediately or store in a covered container in the refrigerator for up to 4 days.

Roasted Grapes

2 pounds [910 g] grapes

2 tablespoons extra-virgin olive oil

1½ tablespoons granulated sugar

Flaky sea salt

Half a lemon (or lime or clementine or mandarin or grapefruit or orange, any citrus really)

Preheat the oven to 400°F [200°C]. Gently wash and dry the grapes, leaving them in bunches on the stems. Transfer to a rimmed baking sheet or baking dish and drizzle with the olive oil. Sprinkle with the sugar and season lightly with salt. Roast until the grapes start to caramelize, about 30 minutes. Squeeze the citrus over the top and set aside to cool. Serve roasted grapes the same day you've roasted them.

ACKNOWLEDGMENTS

This book is the culmination of years of cooking and eating and swimming and marché-ing in Provence-Alpes-Côte d'Azur, paired with even more years of dedicated research during which I cooked and ate and swam and marché-d with an eye toward these pages. I couldn't have done any of it without the help, support, and love of many.

Shooting *le SUD* throughout le sud—from Marseille to Ménerbes to Plascassier—was a dream actualized. JOANN PAI, thank you for trusting me, yet again, and saying yes to photographing book three. You didn't know you were also saying yes to waking up for early morning trains or to climbing the rocks of the calanques and hills of the Luberon with all your gear or to our rental car running out of gas during a national gas shortage, but you did it all and then some in service of getting the shot. To be able to craft a world together, to view and mold it through your lens, and then to revisit it anew in these pages is an extraordinary gift. There will never be enough words or lamb to express how much I value working with you. KATE DEVINE, photography assistant and lifeline, thank you for everything including, quite literally, keeping me alive. I am forever grateful we both took that introvert leap and met for coffee in our early Paris days. Thank you for taking that magic to the south of France with me. Portons un toast à une vie remplie de cafés, de bon vin et de madeleines sans gluten. LISE KVAN, your deft hands, impeccable wine curation, and ridiculously calm presence make shooting on location in unfamiliar kitchens feel like home. Thank you for agreeing to assist *le SUD*, for rescuing us during the aforementioned gas shortage, and for so very much more.

I have a strong emotional attachment to the streets, homes, markets, and tables where we shot *le SUD*. Early on, brainstorming places to visit in order to research this book, I wrote "Julia?" in a notebook and, somehow, through unseen channels, I wound up at La Pitchoune more than once in the making of this book. MAKENNA HELD, thank you for opening your doors and thus, Julia's Provençal doors. To spend a month living, writing, shooting, making my morning coffee, and eventually becoming so comfortable in that iconic pegboarded kitchen that the edges between its past and my present began to fray was a mind trip in the best of ways. Thank you also to KENDALL LANE and CHRIS NYLUND. To JULIA CHILD for setting up that kitchen and so much else, thank you. GWEN STRAUSS, un immense merci for offering us the keys to the rooms and halls and spectacular kitchen of another hallowed home in Ménerbes. La Maison Dora Maar, L'Hôtel de Tingry, and autumn in Provence will forever be linked in my heart. To CÉLIA TUNC, VALÉRIE GILLET, JOËLLE MARTIN, VALENTINA SORBARA, and aux offices de tourisme in the Vaucluse, Apt, Menton, Riviera, Merveilles, and La Brigue, thank you for aiding me in more deeply exploring and discovering your corners of Provence-Alpes-Côte d'Azur. To MAURO COLAGRECO, JULIE MILLET, SILVINA DAYER, and ALESSANDRO DI TIZIO, it was an honor to be immersed in the Mirazur gardens and kitchens and the universe of Menton and Roquebrune-Cap-Martin with you as our guides. Thank you.

Many friends living across le sud opened their tables, their wine cellars, their farms, and the backdoors of their friends and friends of friends. My knowledge and understanding of the region have grown far beyond my initial reach because of you. Un grand merci, particulièrement à JAMIE BECK, LIZA BATTESTIN, EMMANUELLE LUCIANI, DANTE DI CALCE, NADIA SAMMUT, JULIA SAMMUT, JULIA MITTON, LAURA VIDAL, ALEXIS BIJAOUI, MICKAËLLE CHABAT, CATHERINE BASTIDE, and the beautiful La Traverse in Marseille, la merveilleuse équipe at MAISON MOGA in l'Isle-sur-la-Sorgue, and the whole team at LE SAINT HUBERT in Saint-Saturnin-lès-Apt for your kindness and friendship.

I sourced many of the props from brocantes and markets across the south of France. I also sourced from friend's cupboards and kitchens and garages. Thank you especially to my dear amie RUTH RIBEAUCOURT for inviting me to a dinner party and letting me disappear the entirety of apéro in order to pillage her immense yet impeccably curated collection. Thank you, INDIA MILLER, also, for keeping them safe in transit from Lacoste to Ménerbes and back. To SARAH ESPEUTE for making the most spectacular tablecloth and letting me drape it all over the rocks of Marseille.

I love styling my books for many reasons, but one of the biggest is that I get to work with brands I have loved and admired from up close and far away. Thank you to MUUÑ, makers of the finest straw baskets, many of which have carried our market hauls and found their way into these pages. To the incredible talents at MAMO for the spectacular glassware and to PALLARÈS SOLSONA for making my very favorite picnic knives. To the kind humans at HERMÈS, THE FRANKIE SHOP, SESSÙN, LOUP, TOTEME, RSVP PARIS, ILANA KOHN, TUCKER, and TARIK KOIVISTO at Luxe Provence, thank you all for letting me pull from your proverbial closets and play dress up throughout these pages. To INA BEISSNER, merci mille fois for making my dream wedding ring and shipping it directly to Marseille in time for us to use it in our shoot.

IRIS MARCHAND, meeting you in 2015 changed my life completely and forever for the better. Thank you for helping me rediscover and begin to love a part of myself I had hidden. Thank you for meeting us years later during the shooting of this book to picnic and swim and carry melons. And thank you many times over for offering your art in the form of the incredible illustrations that weave through these pages. Merci pour ton investissement incroyable, ton grand coeur, et ton amitié.

Thank you to the friends who have joined me in Provence-Alpes-Côte d'Azur throughout the years and the friends I hope to visit with in the future. THIBAULT CHARPENTIER, for spending many birthdays and nonbirthdays in the Mediterranean and for perfecting my French—même si ce n'est qu'à l'écrit. YASMIN ZEINAB, no words. You are the brightest light, and I can't believe my luck in getting to call you a friend. ALEXIS DEBOSCHNEK, for chatting endlessly about la tropézienne and literally everything else. I value you and our friendship deeply. To JADE ZIMMERMAN for locking eyes with me the first day of pastry school and fifteen years later cross testing many of the recipes in this book. Thank you also for bringing PERIDOT ZIMMERMAN into the/my world. Peri, I can't wait to show you le sud. CAMILLA WYNNE, for letting me text you endless questions about preserving currants. KATY YUNG, for keeping these curls marginally more in check before each shoot. To KORT HAVENS, RYAN HANKE, CYNTHIA NIXON, LINA CASCHETTO, JACKIE KAI ELLIS, SONAL BAINS, TESSA STUART, LIZ CLAYMAN, FARAH KERAM, BEN MIMS, J ANDERSON, SUSAN KORN, EMILY FIFFER, CAT CHEN, and many, many others. Merci, merci, merci.

SARAH BILLINGSLEY, thank you for trusting me and believing in, shepherding, and championing first *À Table* and now *le SUD*. I can't wait to see where we meet for dinner the next time we're even marginally close in the world. Until then, raising my glass and this flawlessly edited book to you. LIZZIE VAUGHAN, thank you for letting me bring my crazy ideas to you, for bringing yours to me, and weaving it all together to create a book that is beyond even my wildest hopes. Working with you is the most fun. I thank you also to JESSICA LING, TERA KILLIP, STEVE KIM, LAUREN HOFFMAN, KEELY THOMAS-MENTER, ELORA SULLIVAN, GABBY VANACORE, and CECILIA SANTINI at Chronicle Books. SARAH SMITH, thank you for your years of guidance, friendship, keen eye, and relentless support of all the dreams I keep bringing your way. I feel as much gratitude in calling you my agent as I do my friend. BLAKE MACKAY, it seems impossible that we have never visited Provence together, and yet you helped me to shape and form and tear out the fantastic from the fantasy while writing this book. Thank you for your precision edits and your sounding boarding and so much more. To SHAB AZMA, JOYCE CAVITT, BROOKLYN HENDERSON, MARKIE JOHANSEN, MAYA DONATO, TAYLOR BRANECKI, and the entire team at ARC Collective, thank you thank you thank you for all you do. Next team lunch in Provence.

To my continuously inspiring mother, DIANE. Thank you for filling my entire lifetime with books and words and support. Thank you also for letting me raid your closet full of striped button-downs and steal your cookie recipe for this book. Sending you an around-the-world hug and already plotting our time in le sud together. MICHAEL SKOGLIND, I snagged a few vintage Ralph Laurens along the way from you too. As you can see in these pages, I've put them to good use. Thank you and also thank you for your endless love and support.

To LAILA AZAR-SAID and RAUL SAID. At no point did anyone tell me that one of the coolest parts of being married was getting to have you as in-laws. Thank you for accepting and welcoming me into your home and lives with such open hearts. Laila, I stole one of your favorite shirts too, thank you. I think of you every time I turn to page 261.

To LAILA SAID, my whole damn heart. Your name runs through this book from dedication to acknowledgments and many a headnote in between for good reason. You were there holding down the towels the day I began conversations for the sale of this book from a windy beach in Ramatuelle. You have driven—and, I'm sure, will drive again—countless rental cars all over le sud during research trips and holidays and holidays turned research trips. You took seven dedicated months out of your life to aid in the research of this book and, as you are wont to do, brought your entire self and then some to the job. You have washed countless dishes, carried an untold number of market bags and props through narrow cobblestone streets and up literal boulders, and then seamlessly transitioned into a swimsuit model. Thank you for reminding me why I write when I need reminding and for championing me when I need championing and for resting with me when I need resting. Thank you for choosing to share this life and for embracing the fact that, at times, the lines blur between work and life and for helping shine light on the beauty and quiet and intention in that blur. This book wouldn't be what it is without your research, your support, your unflagging optimism. This life wouldn't be what it is without you in it. Mi vida, gracias.

Lastly, to the readers joining me in Provence-Alpes-Côte d'Azur through these pages, merci à toutes for reading and cooking and weaving your own stories in. I hope to see you in le sud very soon.

—RKP

INDEX

D

E

F

G

H

I

Strawberry Gâteau 226–28
Sugeli (c/o Madame Maffei) 152–53
syrups
    from candied kumquats 256
    from gueule de bois currants 259
    Mint-Lime Syrup 28
    from poached quince 214

T

tapenade
    Crispy Mushrooms with Tapenade 196
    Tapenade Noire ou Verte 48
tartes
    Tarte à la Raspberry 237–38
    Tarte au Citron 229–31
    Tarte Soleil 69
La Tropézienne 232–35
Tende 152
Tian 178
tisanes 260
tomatoes
    La Bohémienne 177
    La Broufade 131–32
    Cherry Tomatoes with Pistou 167
    Clams + Raïto 108
    Daube Provençal 127–28
    Gazpacho para Ella 199

    Greens with Tomato Vinaigrette 204
    Not Traditional Salade Niçoise 208
    Paella Camarguaise 111–12
    Ratatouille 173–74
    Sandwiches for "Hiking" (Pan Bagnat) 142
    serving perfect in-season 161
    Tarte Soleil 69
    Tian 178
    Tomatade 52
    Tomates à la Provençale 165
    Traditional Salade Niçoise 207
Toulon 78
La Tropézienne 232–35
tuna
    Not Traditional Salade Niçoise 208
    Sandwiches for "Hiking" (Pan Bagnat) 142
    Traditional Salade Niçoise 207

V

van Gogh, Vincent 12, 111
Vd'O 37
vegetables. *See also* **individual vegetables**
    Aïoli, Petit to Monstre 181–82
    Crudité + Beurre Pommade 56
Vence 74

vermouth
    Martini Provençal 32
    Sans Fin 35
vinaigrettes
    Herbed Vinaigrette 203
    Roasted Garlic Vinaigrette 218
    Tomato Vinaigrette 204
vodka
    Vin d'Orange 36

W

walnuts
    Candied Walnuts 82
    Radicchio Salad with Poached Quince 213
wine
    Bendita entre los Melones 225
    La Grande Plage 27
    La Piscine 24

    recommended 40–41
    rosé 40
    Vin d'Orange 36

Z

zucchini
    Pickled Things + Saucisson 70
    Ratatouille 173–74
    Tian 178
    Zucchini Blossoms 65